FULLY QUALIFIED

*Maximizing Your
God-Given Potential*

BABBIE MASON

MASON HILL
BOOKS

FULLY QUALIFIED

Published by Mason Hill Books

A division of Mason Hill Music Group, LLC

P.O. Box 729

Bowdon, Georgia 30108

www.babbie.com

Praises for Fully Qualified

When the old prophet, under the inspiration of the Holy Spirit, wrote "I know the plans I have for you," declares the Lord, "plans to prosper you and not harm you, plans to give you hope and a future," he intuitively perceived something about "God's sovereignty" that we should understand today: God has a plan for our lives. Babble's book is a treatise on the very subject Jeremiah so carefully introduced to anxious hearts centuries ago. This book is not a motivational document. No, **Fully Qualified: Maximizing Your God-given Potential** is "encouragement on steroids." My dear sister provides a step by step plan for knowing, understanding, receiving and implementing God's Plan as HIS "destiny for our lives." Sprinkled throughout the book are wonderful stories, engaging life experiences and practical principles that deal with essentials for Christian living: Authenticity, Excellence, Courage, Leadership, Service, Creativity, Faithfulness, and more. It gives me great pleasure to recommend this book as a resource tool for many years to come. I plan on using **Fully Qualified: Maximizing Your God-given Potential with my students.**

Vernon M. Whaley, Ph.D

Dean - School of Music

Liberty University

Babbie Mason has created a practical, insightful, helpful manual. It is a faith based, scripture laced, God honoring, prayer filled project. There are many "How To" books on the market but this one is highly unique. I am confident it will help to get you where you're going. Babbie is a tried and true, time honored, trusted friend in the CCM world. Known as a consummate lyricist, performer, author, radio show creator, TV talk-show host, and very wise Mama...she is now offering to be our consultant, coach and cheerleader. This book is a gift for anyone who aspires to be **Fully Qualified!**

Ellie Lofaro

Founder, Heart Mind & Soul Ministries

Author/International Speaker

Babbie Mason has written a must-read book for anyone seeking to live an authentic life, be faithful to their gifts and embrace their calling given to them by God. I'm grateful that Babbie has invested in my life and our friendship and believe I am a more authentic leader and friend because of her investment. Fully Qualified: Maximizing Your God-given Potential, will bring readers into a deeper understanding of their purpose enabling them to walk away celebrating their uniqueness based upon the truth of God's Word.

Dr. Peggy Banks

Global Ministry Director

TWR Women of Hope

www.twrwomenofhope.org

———————————————————————————————

Babbie and I have written songs together for over 20 years. Regardless of the genre, she naturally infuses her life-changing words with beauty, eloquence and transparency. Throughout this book, you will encounter Babbie in a way that is up close and personal. She will not only challenge you to be authentic to who God has created you to be, but she also offers meaningful insights on ways to purposefully step away from how culture has defined you, to embrace and exemplify what GOD says about you. This is a must-read for anyone in search of their true-best-self!

Kenn Mann

Producer, Arranger and Dove-Award winning Songwriter

———————————————————————————————

Reading Babbie Mason's book, **Fully Qualified**, reminds me to be just like an old Olive Tree - deeply rooted and grounded, fully persuaded to fulfil my purpose and determined to remain faithful to the Lord.

This book, just like Babbie's singing voice, is a call to action.

Thelma Wells

Award-winning Author and Core Speaker for Women of Faith Conferences

I have had the great blessing to showcase my music and ministry with Babbie Mason through her internet radio station, www.BabbieMasonRadio.com and her television program, Babbie's House. There is no greater friend to the Independent Christian Artist than Babbie Mason. She has offered me such beautiful encouragement and a platform to share my ministry. Because Babbie is an experienced and successful Christian artist and speaker, she has a wealth of insight and knowledge. She has offered me invaluable advice and is incredibly gracious and kind. I would highly recommend her strategies to any Independent Christian Artist. Babbie is an answer to prayer.

Gretchen Keskeys

Independent Recording Artist and Songwriter

I've worked with Babbie Mason for almost 20 years as producer of her show, Babbie's House. I've seen her live what she challenges readers to do in her book, Fully Qualified, and that is to be on a continued quest to develop the unique talents God has given to each of us. In her book, Babbie write, "There is no expiration date on God's plan for your life." That resonates with me and reminds me that we can use our gifts and talents in every season of our lives and be excited about every opportunity that comes our way. You'll be inspired to work with excellence after reading Fully Qualified.

Greg West

President, WATC and Producer of Babbie's House

I love this book! It is the perfect reflection of who Babbie Mason is! We have been friends for decades and I have seen her live out every one of the character traits she points to as important! It's as if she says 'Now, have a seat, my friend, and I'll tell you what you need to know to make it!' You can learn from her, you can depend on her and you will want to re-read her book because it is packed with wisdom, insights, illustrations and valuable practical pointers! If you want to know what makes Babbie Mason great in her field and successful in her life, get out your underlining pen and read **Fully Qualified: Maximizing Your God-given Potential.**

Jan Silvious

Author and Platform Speaker at Women of Faith Conferences

Babbie Mason is the real deal! One only has to listen to her compositions, such as,

The Spirit Is Willing But The Flesh Is Weak or Trust His Heart, watch an episode of Babbie's House, listen to www.BabbieMasonRadio.com, or attend one of her dynamic live events to experience Babbie's love and dedication to God and people. Babbie is secure in her relationship with the Lord Jesus Christ and humble enough to be completely transparent and vulnerable. This book, entitled Fully Qualified is a testament to her leadership. As a result of her coaching, not only do I have my own radio show, I have my own internet radio station!

Brian N. Brooks

(a.k.a. DJ HiPrayze) Host of Joycast on Babbie Mason Radio and founder of DJ HiPrayze Radio

$\mathcal{D}\text{edication}$

To my siblings: Pastor Ben, George Alan, Benita and Matthew. Our mother lovingly referred to us as, "Reverend Wade's Children." She always beamed with joy when she used those words, because she saw the brilliance her children possessed and the genuine pride it brought to our dad. They always saw the best in us. From my place in the middle of five, I think I have the optimal view of their perspective. Your deep faith, love for family and authentic brilliance is what inspires me and lights my way. I love you and dedicate this book to all of you.

Acknowledgements

When thinking of being fully qualified, I immediately reflect on those competent individuals who used their God-given gifts and talents to help me complete this project. It takes a very capable team, and there is no way I could ever say this book was written alone. That team believed in this book long before it was held in our hands. I am tremendously grateful to the following: my husband Charles for being just the kind of man I need. At home or on the road, you've been there to love and lean on. To my personal assistant, Kimberly Hutchins, your numerous gifts are a work of art. Thank you for your tireless service. To photographer, Mitchie Turpin. To make-up artist, Elijah Cohen. To Dr. Fred Jones at Publish Me Now University. You are a blessing to my life. You are challenging me to maximize my talents, venture further into the exploration of my gifts and enlarge my territory. Thank you so much for partnering with me on this journey! To Erika Jones for your faithful assistance, To Editor, Monique Williams and Book Designer, Melodye Hunter, for your beautiful work.

To you, dear reader. I truly hope this book motivates you to use all God has entrusted to you as you endeavor to make Him look good here on earth. In some way, may this book encourage and inspire you to dig deeper into your endless potential to discover more of the richer, fuller, deeper, sweeter life Christ has given you. May you sense God's immense love and my greatest encouragement on every page.

Most of all, I am deeply grateful to my Lord and Savior, Jesus Christ. I acknowledge You as the giver of 'every good and perfect gift.' Because of You, I truly have a song to sing, a story to tell and a reason to celebrate with others. It is a joy to be used for Your glory and honor.

Babbie Mason

IN MEMORY OF MY FATHER

Reverend W. George Wade, 1922-1987

AND IN MEMORY OF MY MOTHER

Georgia Wade, 1923-2015

Table Of Contents

Fully Qualified: Maximizing Your God-Given Potential

Forward

It was a hot, summer, sultry day in Atlanta, Georgia when I went on a mission to the corner grocery with one goal in mind: to find the sweetest, juiciest cantaloupe that money could buy. As I stood before a mound of freshly delivered melon, I embarked upon the age-old ritual of cantaloupe selection by thumping and smelling to find the ripest melon. Suddenly, from behind me came this rich, velvety alto voice making a very pertinent inquiry: "How do they feel," she asked?

As I turned to put a voice with a face, I saw a tall, beautiful, African American pregnant woman. I smiled and responded, "They feel just fine!"

As we struck up a conversation, we discovered that only weeks before, she had sung at my church. However, I was sitting in a distant balcony and from that position she only looked to be about 6 inches tall! She was much taller than that live and up close!

As we chatted, we learned of our mutual love for songwriting. I ran to the car and got her a cassette tape of a few of my compositions and we agreed to make a writing date after the delivery of her baby. We've been writing together ever since!

Over the last thirty- five years, we've penned hundreds of songs. Songs like: All In Favor, The Only Hope, God is Good All The Time, In All of His Glory, What Can Separate You, From Love to Love, Love Like That, King Jesus is His Name, Never Get Enough, Pray On, Christmas with the Ones You Love, and so many more. Even though I wrote, He'll Find a Way, Babbie has sung it all over the world. (I have always considered this song a collaborative effort, too, because Babbie was the first to sing the song. And besides, when I sing it, it doesn't sound like that and no one, hands down, has ever sung He'll Find a Way like she does!)

Through these many years, Bab and I have become more like family than friends. We've been through the deaths of both our dads and in fact she sang at my dad's funeral. Her children call me Auntie D. We've gone through Charles' stroke, Babbie's knee surgery, me having cancer four times and Babbie's mom making her earthly transition into the arms of her Savior. We've vacationed together, had slumber parties during ice storms and we've spent holidays together wearing sweat suits and no bras! (Now that's close!) She sang at Jim's and my wedding, which ushered me into a new season that we had prayed about for years (Isaiah 54) where I became a wife, a mom to three adult children and a Grammy to eleven, all without labor pains!

I felt compelled to share some of our personal history because I would say that other than her husband, her parents and family, I probably know Babbie better than anyone. And here's what I always say of her... whether it's a big opportunity, like performing at Carnegie Hall or on the Billy Graham Crusades, or smaller ones like speaking for a third grader who invited her to come to career day or giving a lift to a stranger she spotted making her way down the road on a walker, I've never known her to ever say no to any ministry prospect.

Always a teacher, mentor and encourager at heart, for decades now, Babbie has held seminars and conferences for aspiring artists and songwriters. She has also taught songwriting at several colleges and universities, always anxious to inspire, equip, direct and offer wisdom to those who are in line to be passed the torch.

For all of these reasons, I'm over the moon excited about this new book, Fully Qualified. It's a manual for our faith walk and service to the Lord. It's a map of encouragement, inspiring you to become all you were designed to be and do all you were created to do. It's a how-to book for figuring out and fulfilling your divine potential.

For many, it will make sense of some of the challenges and difficulties you have faced in life, helping you to embrace the truth that God works everything together for good to those who love Him and are called according to His purpose, even those things we don't get or understand. These pages will help underscore that without preparation, there is no prize and that often times the preparation can be complicated and even overwhelming. However, rather than becoming overwhelmed, there is the choice to trust God and live as an overcomer. Babbie's book, Fully Qualified will remind you to eliminate excuses for not moving forward, and offer great insight and wisdom to help you replace excuses with empowerment and hope.

I believe Fully Qualified will usher in a new season for you. Its message is that important! Real and relevant, it's a life-giving message to all believers, regardless of occupation. When you read, Fully Qualified let its content be an exhortation planted deep in your heart. May hope and confidence rise up on the inside of you as you realize, whatever your earthly assignment, you are well able because the Sovereign God of the Universe has made certain you are Fully Qualified for the days ahead.

Big hugs, Bigger Love,

Donna Douglas Walchle

producer/songwriter/author/speaker

www.donnadhere.com

Fully Qualified

Introduction

FULLY QUALIFIED
Maximizing Your God-given Potential

... giving thanks to the Father who has qualified us

to be partakers of the inheritance of the saints in the light.

Colossians 1:12 NASB

The Apostle Paul wrote the glorious words in the scripture above to the Colossians, teaching them that God has qualified every believer to be a joint heir with all the saints, through Christ Jesus. This ushers every born-again child of God, into a wonderful relationship with Him, Who has already anticipated every need the human race will ever have. In this passage, the Apostle Paul prays that we would fully please God in everything we do, and that we would be fruitful in every good work. He continues to pray that we would increase in the knowledge of God.

The Apostle Paul's fervor increases as he prays that we would live a life that is filled with all God has for us. His love for the church is deeply expressed in prayer as he gives thanks to God who has qualified us to enjoy every blessing He has given His Son, Jesus. Paul desires that we understand that the quality of our spiritual walk is enhanced by our knowledge of God's Word and that this knowledge is the key to opening the door to our personal potential. Recognizing and using our rich potential to honor God, is the only way we can find real joy in life. When we bring glory and honor to God with our lives, we are fulfilling His plan and purpose for each of us.

You see, according to Ephesians 2:10 (AMP), every person God created is a masterpiece, and the great plan and purpose He desires every one of us to fulfill was in place long before we were born. Read this powerful passage.

For we are His workmanship [His own master work, a work of art], created in Christ Jesus [reborn from above—spiritually transformed, renewed, ready to be used] for good works, which God prepared [for us] beforehand [taking paths which He set], so that we would walk in them [living the good life which He prearranged and made ready for us.]

God's master plan for your life didn't just start the day you were born. Long before the beginning, God knew you and planned every day of your life. Psalm 139: 16 (NLT) reveals this.

You saw me before I was born.

Every day of my life was recorded in your book.

Every moment was laid out

before a single day had passed.

There has never been one single moment when you were not in the heart and mind of God. You are not a mistake. You are not an accident or an afterthought. You are not here by chance, but by choice. You have not, nor have you ever been, a surprise to God. Your heavenly Father has always been expecting you and He has always been making plans for you. Even before you were born, God saw who you could become, and He set your life on a trajectory that leads to your fulfillment and His glory. God's purpose for you works in conjunction with your God-given calling, your gifts and talents. God is behind every one of the countless gifts and talents you possess. If you think God blessed you with an abundance of abilities so you could make lots of money just to retire with a nice nest egg, live until your golden years and then pass on to the Great Beyond, you have a sad view of your purpose. God's plan for you is much bigger than that! God gave you unique gifts and talents to be a blessing to others and to glorify Him.

Everything you need to live life to the fullest is already inside of you. You don't need more power. The same spirit that raised Christ from the dead dwells inside of you (Romans 8:11.) You don't need more talent. You were born with an abundance of talent. You don't need more gifts. Your gifts are stored up, just waiting for you to unpack them and use them, according to Romans 12:6. You don't need approval. You are already approved by your heavenly Father. Your personal relationship with Christ establishes that you are already accepted in the Beloved, according to Ephesians 1:6. The power to do exceeding, abundantly, above all you could ask or think, is already at work within you, according to Ephesians 3:20. Your mission, should you decide to accept it – is to align yourself with God's agenda, believing that what He says about you in His Word, is undeniably true. Through your obedience, allow Him to stir up your gifts and talents. Synchronize your faith with God's faithful plan, giving God permission to activate your potential through the power of His Spirit, bringing the best of who you are to the top. In other words, give God something to work with! When you work with God, embracing who you truly are, you can watch God do amazing things in your life! When you discover His plan, dedicating your gifts and talents to fulfill that plan to the glory of God, you will discover what Jesus calls in John 10:10, 'the rich and satisfying life' (NLT).

The word qualified is defined as: fitted (as by training or experience) for a given purpose; competent; having complied with the specific requirements; eligible; to make sufficient, to empower, to authorize. Do you notice that the word qualified in Colossians 1:12 is in the past-tense? This signifies that the act of qualifying has already taken place. This is what God, through Jesus Christ, has already done for you! Not because you've been so good or that you earned the position of qualifying on your own. Everything you have, every gift, every talent, every blessing, even your relationship with God, was given to you, not because you did something to deserve it or that you earned it, but because God loves you and saw fit to bestow upon you every blessing He gave to His beloved Son, Jesus, according to Ephesians 2:8-9. To fully realize this position, you must completely surrender your life to God, accepting His Son, Jesus as Savior, believing you were created to bring Him glory with your life according to Revelation 4:11. This is the very moment your best life begins.

In my 34 years of ministry as a singer, teacher, songwriter, author, speaker, TV talk show host, communications pioneer, mentor and success coach, I can honestly say that I get to do what I love and I love what I do. It's not because I am so smart and could figure it all out. The complete opposite is true. I can't take any credit for anything the Lord has done for me. If any good has come of my life, it's been because God is so generous with His love, and He saw fit to use me. In and of myself there is nothing to applaud. I am deeply flawed. I tend to be perfectionistic, impulsive and I struggle to stay in step with the Lord. But this keeps me humble and desperately dependent on the Him. I know He still desires to use me, and I know my best days are still out in front of me.

Here's what's interesting. I've always wanted to be a singer and a teacher. I've been singing all my life and went into the teaching profession straight out of college. But the remaining occupations in the list above have taken me by complete surprise. I didn't set out to be a songwriter, author, public speaker or a TV talk show host. But God saw all of that and He put the potential in me. Then He gave me the desire. He called it out of me. Then He gave me the ability and the opportunity. God did it all! And the powerful truth is - as long as I live, I will have endless gifts, talents and potential to use for God - gifts and talents that bring joy and meaning to life! With God, your potential is never at a deficit. Whatever you wanted to be, ever since you were a kid, was only the beginning. You have gifts and talents you don't even know you have. There is a wealth of endless possibility already stored up on the inside of you just waiting to be realized. While many people go through life never discovering their true potential, you must choose to acknowledge God's power on the inside of you. Yes, you may become overwhelmed, thinking you have to step up your game and compete with the guy in the lane next to you. You may even want to quit before you can get started. Here's the key. It's not about you. Go ahead and let yourself off the hook. You can't do anything within your own power. But you can do great things with God's power at work in you. You have endless potential. Your first step is to believe it.

Do you know where an abundance of the earth's talent is laid to rest? In the graveyard! So many people have died with their gifts, talents and dreams untapped. Maybe they were trapped by a feeling of hopelessness that discouraged them. Maybe they were unmotivated or got stuck in life. Maybe they were overwhelmed by their circumstances, and the circumstances won out. Whatever the reason, they allowed their gifts to lie dormant and their dreams to die within them. In fact, of the 7.5 billion people on the earth, very few of them will maximize their full potential. Most people are satisfied with mediocrity. They are not even aware of the latent power that lies deep within them. That is where your potential comes on to the scene.

The root of the word potential is potent. If something is potent, it is innately strong, laden with power, effective, persuasive and compelling. Some people don't like the word potential because it's not something tangible you can hold in your hand. It suggests something uncontainable or unreachable, way out there in the distance. But that is precisely why I love the word. When you recognize your potential, you'll come to the realization that you are never out of resources, ideas, options or possibilities. Can you see yourself overflowing with an endless supply of resources? Do you desire to maximize the power within you to live out the true purpose for which you were born? Are you ready to glorify God and be a blessing to the world? If your answer is yes, then it's time you tapped into your endless potential, pursuing that unique call upon your life with vigor and passion.

One of my biggest dreams in life is to help you live yours. I believe by reading this book you'll be reminded not to settle in the land of mediocrity when an endless realm of possibility is within your reach. I'm not implying I'm all that or that this book holds all the answers. I only want to remind you that I'm with you on the journey. Yes, we are mighty alone, but we are mightier when our faith is joined with another. You see, success is just a little farther down the road from failure. If you desire to do anything for God, you'll need a coach to challenge you, a counselor to advise you, a champion to fight for you. a warrior to pray for you, and a cheering squad to remind you not to quit on your dreams. In the music ministry and industry, so many people are not willing to share what they know, as if, by empowering you, they somehow become less powerful. The complete opposite is true! Empowerment does not mean that I step on you or over you on my way to success. It means I grab your hand and bring you with me. By doing that, both of us are better. Information is powerful, but it's more powerful when connected with experience. I don't know much, but what I do know, it's a privilege to share with you.

Are you ready? All of heaven is behind you. God is ready, willing and able to use you in ways you've only dreamed of. You are pre-qualified for any tasks that await you. If you'll give Him permission, God will open doors of opportunity for you and use you to change your world.

~

Preface

BEFORE YOU BEGIN

It doesn't seem like it, but I am nearing the age when many of my counterparts are thinking of retiring. Honestly speaking, it seems the older I get, the more energized I become. The days ahead for me prove to be more exciting than ever. New and fresh assignments from God continue to come my way. I believe I have found my sweet spot. This doesn't mean that I don't get physically tired. Trust me. There are days when I am so tired, all I can do is move from the bed to the sofa and back to the bed. But the work I do is not toil. It's a labor of love. At this season of my life I still get to do what I enjoy. Retirement is not on my agenda. According to Dr. Myles Munroe's book, Living With Purpose, retirement is not on God's agenda either. He says, "You were not designed to retire. You came out of God and God hasn't retired. He's been working ever since He spoke the invisible into the visible. Therefore, retirement is not a part of His plan for your life. Because God created man by giving him an immortal spirit, with eternal potential, God planned enough work to keep you busy forever. Oh, you may retire from a specific organization or job, but you never retire from life and work. The minute you quit working, you begin to die, because work is a necessary part of life. "

As someone who wants to use all my gifts for God, I continue to find great joy in the learning and discovery process. For me, that process is basically chronicled in decades. For instance, in the 60's I was in basic training, developing necessary skills. In the 70's I graduated from school and began my career. In the 80's I embarked upon classroom teaching, songwriting and studio recording. In the 90's I began to spread my wings as a concert artist, author and public speaker. In the new millennium, I was introduced to ways technology could help me efficiently and effectively produce and perpetuate my work. After 2010, it became explicitly clear that I was to use the culmination of my gifts and experiences to prepare and equip the next generation of creative thinkers for the future. God is not finished with me yet! There's an old African proverb that says, "He is a fool who thinks he knows everything." I'll be the first to admit that even after fifty plus years of learning, there is so much I still don't know. I will always be a student. The joy is in the journey, not in just reaching the destination. As a perpetual student, I am still easily inspired. I don't think it's even possible to use up all of our potential. The very moment I think I've run out of ideas or come to the end of my ability, God gives more ideas and more strength even until it overflows. While others my age may consider retiring, I'm going to keep re-firing because I don't want to miss anything God has for me! Grab hold of that! As long as you walk with God you will never, ever be depleted of resources.

There are many people in my life who have inspired me and contributed to who I am. I'll pass on some of the wisdom, knowledge, ministry motivation and encouragement I've gleaned from them. And there are people in the Bible who have also inspired me because of their deep passion for God. David, the son of Jesse, is one of those people who continues to motivate me. He represents particular virtues I find not only admirable, but also necessary for success. In each chapter, we will try to learn something from David's life, for he embodies the character qualities that every ministry-minded believer, who desires to excel in ministry, business and life, should possess. Let's take a moment to look at his story.

The story of David's calling and anointing as king of Israel is found in 1 Samuel 16:1-13. The prophet Samuel visited the house of Jesse to choose Israel's king from among Jesse's sons. One by one, each of Jesse's sons passed before the Prophet

Samuel. And one by one, each son was rejected. Then, in verse 11, the prophet said to Jesse, "Are all thy children here? And he said, There remaineth yet the youngest, and behold, he keepeth the sheep. And Samuel said unto Jesse, 'Send and fetch him: for we will not sit down till he come hither.' And he sent, and brought him in. Now he was ruddy and of a beautiful countenance and goodly to look to. And the LORD said, "Arise, anoint him: for this is he." KJV

Samuel immediately saw David's qualifications. But for whatever reason, David was not his father's choice. Just a rough-cut teenager who, no doubt, had the musty smell of animals and the out-of-doors about him, David was in the pasture keeping his father's sheep when Jesse's choicest older sons were paraded before the Prophet Samuel. But, David was certainly God's first choice. You see, God favors the unlikely, the unassuming, the unnoticed, even the underdog to carry out His plan and purpose, so that His name and His kingdom may ultimately be advanced. Verse 13 reveals some of the most beautiful words ever spoken about any man.

"And the spirit of the Lord came upon David from that day forward."

You see, man may overlook your potential. Even those closest to you may take you for granted, missing the gold mine that lies within you. But God sees you! And He is pleased to use you to accomplish His purposes through your life and destiny. Don't be distracted by the fact that people don't validate you. They can't see your value through the currency of their own pain. Jealousy, envy and comparison may prevent them from seeing all you have to offer. You, on the other hand, know that your pain is not in vain. The greater the pain, the greater the gain! Everything the enemy has used to try and set you back, God will turn it around and use that very thing to launch you into your next season.

While David was still at home keeping his father's sheep, God was defining his destiny. Everything David needed to be successful was already inside of him. Before he ever left the sheep's pasture, God had already decided the trajectory of David's life starting with the place where David would begin his first ministry assignment. Likewise, you can't ever be satisfied to remain where you are. David was a good shepherd boy, but he was a great king. The same is true of you. God has already laid out a path for you. Find it and get on it. That path leads to your success. Don't worry about the qualifications. God has already qualified you. You already have whatever it's going to take. You have the potential. You have the gifts and the talents. You have God's help. You only need to discover God's plan, dare to realize your potential, prepare yourself and go to work. Only when you work in tandem with God, will you find your sweet spot, tap into your gold mine and turn dreams into a reality.

One day, as I was reading the remaining verses of 1 Samuel 16:14-23, my eyes were opened to the amazing qualities David possessed. These qualities are what qualified David for ministry. They could be described as personal attributes, personality traits, natural giftedness and spiritual endowments. All of these qualities made him desirable to God and man. It's these qualifications we will highlight in this book.

Let's take a look at the passage. I want you to become familiar with each verse of the story. If you are ministry-minded, a creative thinker, success oriented or a big dreamer, lean in, tune your heart and read purposefully.

14 Now the Spirit of the LORD departed from Saul, and an evil spirit from the LORD terrorized him. 15 Saul's servants then said to him, "Behold now, an evil spirit from God is terrorizing you. 16 Let our lord now command your servants who are before

you. Let them seek a man who is a skillful player on the harp; and it shall come about when the evil spirit from God is on you, that he shall play the harp with his hand, and you will be well." 17 So Saul said to his servants, "Provide for me now a man who can play well and bring him to me." 18 Then one of the young men said, "Behold, I have seen a son of Jesse the Bethlehemite who is a skillful musician, a mighty man of valor, a warrior, one prudent in speech, and a handsome man; and the LORD is with him." 19 So Saul sent messengers to Jesse and said, "Send me your son, David, who is with the flock." 20 Jesse took a donkey loaded with bread and a jug of wine and a young goat, and sent them to Saul by David, his son. 21 Then David came to Saul and attended him; and Saul loved him greatly, and he became his armor bearer. 22 Saul sent to Jesse, saying, "Let David now stand before me, for he has found favor in my sight." 23 So it came about whenever the evil spirit from God came to Saul, David would take the harp and play it with his hand; and Saul would be refreshed and be well, and the evil spirit would depart from him. NASB

As we unpack these verses, note how these qualifications pertain to your personal life and your public ministry. It doesn't matter what you do for a living. If you are a believer in Jesus, then you are in full-time ministry and everything you do makes a difference. If you desire to achieve success in any endeavor, it will be vitally important to assess where you are now so you'll be eligible to graduate to the next level of your God-given assignment. On God's agenda, nothing is ever wasted. We'll make it a point to even glean from our mistakes as well as our successes.

My prayer, as you read, is that you'll gain some insight into your earthly assignment. Hopefully, you'll discover more concerning your purpose and God's plan as you consider all God has given you and all He wants to do in your life. In a very significant way, I believe God will use these words even to provoke you. Not to do more. That only leads to exhaustion. But to be more. That leads to joy and fulfillment. There is a reason God brought you to this planet. He's already called you. It's time you answered that call and seized your moments to walk in your God-given destiny.

Now, as you read, there are some things I want you to prayerfully consider. First, embrace the truth that there is a calling on your life. The Bible says in 2 Peter 1:10, Therefore, brothers, be all the more diligent to confirm your calling and election, for if you practice these qualities you will never fall.

God has something He wants you to do! Your responsibility is to ready yourself with skill, equip yourself with knowledge, broaden your experiences, seek reputable counsel, expose yourself to diverse training, saturate your life with prayer, and do whatever is necessary to fulfill your calling, purpose or undertaking. God could use anything He wanted to promote His cause in the earth. But He chooses to use you!

Next, I challenge you to dream big. Casting convention aside, imagine going where you've never gone before. Don't worry about how you'll do it, just let the ideas flow. If you had the money, the talent and the assistance you needed, what would you set out to do? Write a book? Record a music project? Speak before an audience? Launch a business? Invent a product? Impact more people? Explore uncharted territories? The power is already within you! You are already qualified! Begin by setting some goals. Take inventory of the first three or four things you need to do and the people you'll need to help you get there. As ideas come to you, don't treat them casually. Ponder each idea and treat it as valid, while envisioning your rise to the next level. Don't sell yourself short, but starting where you are right now, embrace your gifts and talents. Time is out for procrastination. Dreaming of the possibilities, endeavor to use whatever gift you have in your hand – right now.

The third thing I'll encourage you to do is prepare for success. Faith makes things possible, that doesn't mean things will be easy. You're qualified, but you'll need to know how to use your qualifications. Success never happens by accident. It's not about greatness or making a name for yourself. Success is about endurance. Keep putting one foot in front of the other until you finish. As the old saying goes, "Plan your work, then work your plan." Don't worry if you encounter difficulty. Expect difficulty. The battle you are experiencing may be challenging, but the reward promises to be worth it.

Here's the fourth thing I'll ask you to do. Write your ideas down! I believe as you read, great ideas will begin to flow. As thoughts come to you, don't just say, "Wow, that was nice idea." Capture the moment and write it down. Keep a journal nearby to record the inspirations and bright ideas you are sure to receive while reading this book. Great readers make great writers. Together, reading and writing are like priming a pump. At first, the ideas may be a little slow at coming. But before long, the inspirations will flow so prolifically, you'll not be able to write fast enough. Your ideas may keep you up at night and distract you from your work by day. That is all a part of the creative process. Take it as it comes. Pay attention to creative impulses and imaginative nudges. Waste nothing. Even the shortest brainstorm could open the door to your biggest idea. So, put your heart and soul into the smallest inspiration. Write down any inspirations for songs or books, business ideas and quotes that speak to your heart as you read. Some of your best songs and book ideas will originate from your own personal journal entries. This discipline may seem insignificant now, but over time, a collection of written notes, inspiring quotes, and divine ideas could be the spark you need for your next project or assignment.

Here's the last thing I'll ask of you. Pray that as you read this book, the Lord, through His spirit will speak to your heart. Whenever we read and ponder God's Word, a spiritual seed is planted. A seed takes root, sprouts a shoot, and in due season, bears fruit. The Apostle Paul's prayer in Colossians 1:9-12 really sums it up so powerfully.

9For this reason we also, since the day we heard it, do not cease to pray for you, and to ask that you may be filled with the knowledge of His will in all wisdom and spiritual understanding; 10 that you may walk worthy of the Lord, fully pleasing Him, being fruitful in every good work and increasing in the knowledge of God; 11 strengthened with all might, according to His glorious power, for all patience and longsuffering with joy; 12 giving thanks to the Father who has qualified us to be partakers of the inheritance of the saints in the light. NKJV

As you pray, believe. Believe that God can do in us what He did in David. In and of ourselves we will never measure up. We deserve death and eternal separation from God. But because of what Jesus did for us at the cross, we don't get what we deserve. We get what Jesus deserves. He has already qualified us to share in His inheritance. That is good news! Ask God to speak specifically to your heart, stirring up your gifts and using His Word to change you from the inside out. Remember, it's not the truth you know, but the truth you obey that makes a difference. As you step out in obedience, the Lord promises to honor your obedience with more opportunity.

At the end of each chapter, I will lead you in a Call To Action. Deliberately ponder each challenge and ask God to show you how to personally carry out each charge in your own life. Read each prayer aloud, endeavoring to agree with the focus of each prayer. Feel free to add to each prayer as you are led.

I'm praying even now that the Spirit of God will stir you up on the inside and cause visions, dreams and desires for your future to germinate and take shape. God is the author of amazing things and He wants to use you to accomplish them. Get ready to put your talents into action. Launch the music ministry. Write your best-selling books. Activate your dream of getting into radio, television or motion pictures. Consider enrolling in that college course or starting the new business! As you read this book, believe that your best inspirations will be revealed. Expect the unexpected. Believe the extraordinary. Predict the unpredictable. Imagine the uncommon happening in your life. Your best days are not behind you. Your best and brightest days are still out in front of you. I believe in you. More than that, God believes in you. He believed in you before you believed in yourself. And He's ready to take you higher, to the next level, to places you've only imagined you could go.

CHAPTER 1

◇◇◇◇◇◇◇◇◇◇◇◇◇◇◇◇◇◇◇◇◇◇◇◇◇◇◇

BE AUTHENTIC

*Behold, I have seen a son of Jesse, the
Bethlehemite . . . 1 Samuel 16:18*

Do you know that you have more creative power, more gifts and talents, and more boundless potential than you could ever use in a lifetime?

Imagine your potential being like a vast sky with an endless horizon or a boundless ocean as wide as it is deep. You possess a perpetual wealth of promise and possibility with an incredible capacity to create the life God desires you to have. You may find that difficult to believe, but it's totally true. You may be discouraged by past failures or paralyzed by an uncertain future, unable to move forward. It could be that your personal inner fears hold you hostage, convincing you that you don't have what it takes to be successful. What speed bumps trip you up, causing you to think you're all maxed out or that your life won't get any better than it is right now? The answer is not 'out there somewhere', but inside of you. One of the biggest battles you'll ever face in life is the intense battle for your identity. Embracing your true authenticity begins with what you think about yourself. The real authentic person you truly are is not defined by the culture. Your identity is not in what people call you. It's not in what you do for a living or in your social status. The real you is defined by God, who created you.

There are six generations living on the earth right now. Each generation has similar characteristics and traits they commonly share. The GI Generation, for example, includes those born between 1901 and 1926. They are strongly dedicated to personal morality and have an extremely high standard of right and wrong. Known as The Greatest Generation, they endured the the Great Depression and The Great War, and are dedicated to God and country. Marriage was for life. Divorce was rare and having children out of wedlock was frowned upon. The Silent Generation includes people who were born between 1925-1945, and are known for their traditional values, their strong work ethic and their caution to speak freely against the establishment and the issues of their day, such as the war, poverty and political issues at that time. As children, they were seen and not heard. As adults, they kept private matters private, and their pain neatly concealed behind their masks as they went on with their lives. Baby Boomers, those born between 1946 and 1964 are considered the wealthiest up to their generation. They are considered the most physically fit and the most optimistic group. They married young, started families and were confident that the future would be brighter than it was for their parents. Younger generations, Generation X and Millennials are known for being more open-minded and liberal than past generations. They are said to be the most educated generation in Western history and as a result are more expressive and opinionated. They are said, on the other hand, to be irresponsible, have high feelings of entitlement, coddled by their parents and are known for 'keeping it real' all over the internet through social media as they divulge the details of their private lives, complete with photographs and videos.

While generations have certain traits and are defined by certain characteristics, we must not lump everyone into the same bag or throw the baby out with the bathwater, so to speak. I want to encourage you to dismiss what 'they say'. 'They' have been known to be wrong. And 'they' are very often wrong about you! True authenticity is really the antithesis of going with the cultural flow. Authenticity is basically, dying to self and one's personal desires. It is laying down the person others think we are, the person we think we are and the person we want others to think we are, to embrace who God truly created us to be. Yes, authenticity is the transparency and admission of weakness or failure. It is the rejection of anything hypocritical or pretentious. But to be truly authentic, you must be willing to celebrate what makes you uniquely different from everyone else on the planet. And you must be totally comfortable with who you are. God's people can be authentic in the truest sense because everything we say and do should be based upon the truth of God's Word. Regardless of when or where you were born, there is a call on your life to do something in a way that has never been done before. Regardless of the economy, what war erupted during your lifetime, who was president when you were a child, what your parents did for a living, or whether you grew up in the city, the suburbs or in a rural setting, you were born one of a kind. There

> *God's people can be authentic in the truest sense because everything we say and do should be based upon the truth of God's Word.*

has never been, nor will there ever be another you. You were born at precisely the right moment in history - for such a time as this. I Peter 2:9 says, "But you are a chosen race, a royal priesthood, a holy nation, a people for his own possession, that you may proclaim the excellencies of him who called you out of darkness into his marvelous light."

To be truly authentic doesn't mean we have to 'keep it real', airing our dirty laundry for dirty laundry's sake, defiling those around us with the gruesome details of our personal lives. True authenticity means we use our purpose, our passion and our pain to empower others. When others know they are not alone on the journey, the one who shares encouragement finds just as much strength as the one who receives it. The quintessential positive thinker, Zig Ziglar shared with keen transparency of how he struggled to practice the positive message he preached for so many years after a fall down a flight of stairs. Dealing with the daily challenges of a head injury, he continued to raise others up with his perpetual honesty and optimism.

In his book, Embrace The Struggle, he said, "The first person you have to be transparent with at all times is yourself. If you can't see what is going on with you, you can't see what needs to happen next. The alcoholic who doesn't think she has a drinking problem won't seek help. The workaholic who denies that twelve-hour work days are too long won't take time off to see his child's soccer game. The perfectionist can't and won't relax, the morbidly obese won't get healthy, and the people who think they present a perfect picture to the whole world will take themselves way too seriously. The list is endless...add a few of your own... maybe you'll discover something that applies to you."

American pastor, author and radio personality, Charles Swindoll said this, "I know of nothing more valuable, when it comes to the all-important value of authenticity, than simply being who you are." The only way you can truly glorify God with your life to live effectively is to embrace your true self. If you go through life never fully accepting who you really are, or embracing your true identity, you will never fulfill your destiny. God's desire for us is to be comfortable just being ourselves. People who are their real, transparent, authentic selves are confident in who God created them to be.

When you are confident in who God made you to be, you can be comfortable, without apology, in your own skin.

Jeremiah 1:5 says "Before you were conceived in your mother's womb, God knew you." This means that before you were born, God knew you intimately and designed you with potential, possibility, and promise. Your gifts, talents, your looks, the texture of your hair, the size of your nose, your likes, dislikes, your personality, all contribute to your divine design. When you know your life has meaning and purpose and that you were created on purpose, with purpose and for a purpose, you can easily celebrate yourself without being boastful on one hand or self-conscious on the other. When you are confident in who God made you to be, you can be comfortable, without apology, in your own skin. **To maximize your God-given potential as a person with unique gifts and talents, you must live an authentic, purposeful life through a personal relationship with God – the Giver of your potential.**

King David was the perfect balance between tough and tender. He was a musician, yet he was a warrior. He was a gentle shepherd, yet he killed wild animals with his bare hands. He composed original songs and played the harp, yet he could pick off a giant with a sling and a single stone. In the same way, you are unique, possessing the perfect balance of the celestial and the terrestrial. God created you to be heavenly minded, yet you have the potential to do earthly good because God endowed you with a plethora of gifts and talents to be used to impact the whole

Don't run from your uniqueness – embrace it. Your uniqueness is your superpower!

world. That uniqueness you have – that ingredient that sets you apart from the rest of humanity, is the key to your strength. Don't run from your uniqueness – embrace it. Your uniqueness is your superpower! Basically, to be authentic is to be at home with yourself, to be true to yourself and your values. That doesn't mean you have God's permission to 'do your own thing'. But you do have His permission to 'do your own thing' within the unimaginable boundaries of His will. The life God has planned for you begins with owning your unique set of strengths, gifts and talents. When you look outwardly at what others are doing, desiring what they have, you will become greatly distracted. You'll be tempted to compare yourself to others. You'll seek their affirmation, falling short of your purpose. You'll focus on your weaknesses, bringing on discouragement and self-doubt. Do you see how this leads to a set-back? Instead, find the validation you need in God. This is where your true identity originates. You must never hesitate to embrace your true, authentic self. I'll remind you of what God told the Prophet Samuel when he was looking for Israel's next king. "Man looks at the outward appearance, but God looks at the heart." (I Samuel 16:7). Seeing yourself as God sees you opens the door to true fulfillment and joy.

I struggled for many years to be at peace with who I am, particularly as it pertains to my musical style. My father, the late, great Reverend W. George Wade was the founding pastor of the Lily Missionary Baptist Church in Jackson, Michigan. I was the full-time church pianist and choir director, hired at age 9 and played for the church for almost 20 years. I grew up singing the traditional Black gospel music of the 60's and 70's. The songs of Mahalia Jackson, Roberta Martin, the Consolers, the Caravans and the Sensational Nightingales defined the music of my early childhood. As I approached my 20's and began to spread my wings as a musician, my style became less traditional and more contemporary, more middle of the road. As a budding solo singer, I emulated the style of both Black and White singer-songwriters. Blaring from my record player in my small, second-floor apartment, you'd hear the music of Andrae Crouch, Danniebelle Hall, Edwin and Walter Hawkins, Beverly Glenn, Evie Tornquist, Second Chapter of Acts and Honeytree. Later on when I began singing and recording professionally, I wrote and recorded ballads such as All Rise, Each One Reach One, Standing in The Gap, With All My Heart, God Has Another Plan, To The Cross, Pray On, In All of His Glory and Trust His Heart, among others. People would often hear my music on the radio and assume I was a White woman. Then they would come to my concerts and be surprised to find that I was Black. Honestly speaking, that used to mess with my head. I felt that I was weird or a misfit. I was convinced that my music sounded too white for Black people and too black for White people. I felt inadequate about my music and self-conscious about my voice. I felt as though I were gray.

Over time, however, I began to see something unique and beautiful occurring in my concerts. From the stage as I was performing, I'd look out over the audience and see a beautiful blend of the body of Christ represented consistently in the audiences that attended my concerts. It was and still is a beautiful thing to see different races, denominations and cultures coming together in worship. Back in those days, on many occasions, I was the first Black person ever to sing in many White churches. And, in many cases, a blended gathering of believers had never taken place in those churches until they opened their doors to a Babbie Mason Concert. God used and is still using this ministry as a bridge to bring people together in worship instead of a category that keeps people polarized.

The very moment I began to celebrate the distinct quality of my voice and the unique calling God has placed on my life, was the very moment I truly began to walk in my destiny and calling. In my experience, the very thing we think is strangest about us, is the very thing God wants to use to set us apart and establish our greatness. What we consider a weakness, God will use to show Himself strong. I thank God for those who showed me

> *Don't ever apologize to others for your uniqueness. You see, God did not create you to blend in among the masses. He created you to stand out!*

the way. I praise God for their music. Those artists I mentioned and many, many more that I didn't, were excellent role models for me. But eventually, I had to make my own way and be true to my own self and God's plan for me. That's what I'm saying to you. Take the risk and step out in your uniqueness. Don't settle for a watered down version of yourself or put limits on your potential. If you are busy trying to be a copycat of someone else, then who will represent you? If two people are the same, one of them will be unnecessary. When I have duplicate files in my computer, my computer will let me know so I can keep the original file and delete the copy to save space. Do you see the power and the importance in being your own beautiful self? Don't ever apologize to others for your uniqueness. You see, God did not create you to blend in among the masses. He created you to stand out!

At the heart of authenticity is a balanced life. The key to finding the right balance is exhibited through your character – those foundational qualities of the mind and heart that one possesses based on morals, honor and principle. Godly character is doing the right thing, at the right moment, using the right method, with the right motive. Character is who you really are, not who others think you are. I heard someone say that character is who you are when no one else is looking. Let me add one thing to that. God is always looking! Character, exhibited through your actions, is built from a real, intimate, vibrant personal relationship with Jesus at the center, as Savior and Lord. Godly character will keep your life on course. God has placed your life on a trajectory of purpose and intention. If your life is off course one degree today, where will you be in one year, in five years or a decade from now? Plain and simple, godly character originates from the heart of God and determines the decisions and choices you make. God is looking for real people of great moral character. These character traits are a byproduct of your underlying beliefs and values. Simply put, what you believe will determine how you live your life.

If you're at peace with who God made you to be, there will be no need to covet or secretly desire the gift or talent someone else may have. You see, when I'm confident in who God called me to be, I will have absolutely no problem celebrating who you are. In fact, I can become your biggest cheerleader. What you have doesn't propose a threat to me at all. I can just be myself, allowing you to see my flaws and imperfections. You may know people who are threatened by what you do or the opportunities you may have. They may feel jealous or envious of you when it appears that God is using you more than He appears to be using them. That mentality comes from putting confidence in the flesh. That mindset derives from self-confidence, which is shallow, petty and vulnerable. We cannot, for even a moment, trust the flesh, its motives or anything it does. Philippians 3:3 says this. "For we are the circumcision, which worship God in the spirit, and rejoice in Christ Jesus, and have no confidence in the flesh".

What difference should it make then, who God chooses to use as long as He receives the glory and His kingdom is advanced? What we should really desire is God-confidence. Psalm 115:1 says," Not to us, LORD, not to us but to your name be the glory, because of your love and faithfulness". NIV. With God-confidence, we can lift each other up and pray for one another's success. After all, aren't we all on the same team? When we have this mindset, God will cheer us on and bring us success.

As you read 1 Samuel 16, did you notice that the conversation the servant had with King Saul concerning David, took place initially without David's knowledge? Do you see how good character can open a door? The possibility is great, that even right now your name is being brought up in a conversation somewhere. Your spouse, your family members, someone at work, church, place of recreation, a local shop or store – somewhere someone may be mentioning your name as a result of an encounter with you. This reveals the fact that people are taking notes on you - always and in all ways. Up close or from a distance, people are checking you out. They may have already drawn conclusions about you based on your character. Is that a sobering thought to you? It should be!

Therefore, if it's a possibility that your name could be spoken in a conversation somewhere at any moment, what could possibly be said about you? Is your name being spoken of in a favorable light? People may say things like, "He really has a servant's heart." "She has the sweetest disposition." "I've never heard him say a negative word." "She is a very loyal and trustworthy friend." "I love her voice. She sings like an angel." "He is a gifted communicator." Are people saying those kinds of things about you? Or could the opposite be true? Is it possible people are saying things like "He's a nice guy, but he uses bad language." "She's never on time. She'll be late to her own funeral!" "He's a slacker. He tries to get by with doing less." "She's difficult to work with." "He thinks it's all about him." "He has a short temper and flies off the handle easily." Could comments such as these be what people are saying about you? I hope not! You see, people are looking for any reason at all to disqualify you. Sad to say, but there are people who do not want you to succeed, so don't contribute to their agenda. The very thought of your success, intimidates them. But, praise God, there are people who believe in you and are depending on you. Because others are in step behind you, you must live, as the Bible says, 'above reproach.' If you are aware of personal character flaws, with the help of God, you can put an end to them today.

Everything Saul's servant had to say about David was favorable. Saul's servant had been taking serious notes on David. The servant and David were probably close friends. Maybe they were schoolmates or their families resided in the same neighborhood. What's remarkable here, is that the servant knew David well enough to know his character. He described David's behavior, his abilities and his appearance in great detail and because of that one conversation, David was called into the service of the king.

How does David's story apply to you? There are people with whom you come in contact on a daily basis who have formulated opinions and drawn conclusions of you strictly based on your character. They could be people you know well or someone you know through your church or at work. They may recognize your leadership abilities and

Your character could open doors for you at any moment, so make sure your character aligns with your calling.

recommend you for job advancement. Your neighbors may remark about how well your lawn is manicured and recommend that you serve on a neighborhood watch team. Church or ministry staff members may remark about how much they enjoyed your recent solo or sermon and conclude that you would make a good ministry leader. Other parents may confer together to ask you to join the school advisory council based on your loyalty and support for the school. Do you see how your name could be the subject of many conversations? Your authentic behavior and your godly character are deciding factors, drawing others to you. Your character could open doors for you at any moment, so make sure your character aligns with your calling. Wherever you go, arrive with Jesus! I'll tell you what I told my own children when they were small. God wants you to have character, not be a character.

There is a great lesson to learn here. While gifts and talents are bestowed, character is developed. Author of Madame Butterfly, John Luther said this, "Good character is more to be praised than outstanding talent. Most talents are to some extent, a gift. Good character, by contrast, is not given to us. We have to build it piece by piece, by thought, choice, courage and determination."

A few years ago, I received a phone call that seemed to come out of the blue. The young man on the other end of the phone announced his name and told me that he worked for a major publishing company in Nashville, Tennessee. Then he said, "Our company is developing a new line of books. Your name came up in our meeting today and we'd like to know if you'd like to write a book for us." There have been times when I have written lengthy book proposals and then hoped that the proposal got a shot with publishers. But this time the prospect came knocking at my door. That began a long relationship with Abingdon Press. The first book I wrote for the company is called, Embraced By God. The company loved the book and developed a women's Bible study by the same name. Another book, This I Know For Sure, was published, along with another companion Bible study. A third book, I Am A Daughter Of The Most High King was released. Soon after the release of Embraced By God, I began to receive requests to speak at women's conferences and retreats. Today I am speaking from the stage almost as much as I am singing. I don't know what was said in that meeting the morning the gentleman from the publishing company called me. But, I believe my character and reputation arrived before that conversation ever took place. I like what preacher and author, Dr. Dwight L. Moody said. "If I take care of my character, my reputation will take care of me."

There is no expiration date on God's plan for your life. Your best days are still ahead of you.

I don't tell you all of that to boast. The Lord knows and I will confess that I am by no means perfect. As I mentioned before, I am a work in progress. But, deep within my heart, I desire to please the Lord with my life, my gifts and talents. By the grace of God, after 34 years in ministry,

I'm still here, enjoying new and exciting assignments. Just as the Bible says, my gifts are still making room for me. There is no expiration date on God's plan for your life. Your best days are still ahead of you. Every one of those ministry opportunities I just described came my way as God opened doors for me. After three decades, the phone is still ringing. As we endeavor to pursue our God-given calling, work hard at developing our skills, remaining true to who God has called us to be, and we realize that what we do is not about money, but it's about God and people, God will go out of His way to honor our lives with good things.

Romans 12:1-2 says this.

> And so, dear brothers and sisters, I plead with you to give your bodies to God because of all he has done for you. Let them be a living and holy sacrifice—the kind he will find acceptable. This is truly the way to worship him. Don't copy the behavior and customs of this world, but let God transform you into a new person by changing the way you think. Then you will learn to know God's will for you, which is good and pleasing and perfect. NLT

God is looking for someone who is real and genuine; someone who will always be honest with themselves. It is so important to do your own reality check every now and then. That honest assessment, along with good moral character will help you to represent His kingdom everywhere you go. You must believe that God has given you desirable qualities that are attractive to others. In a world full of tricksters and imposters, He's searching for people who are comfortable just being themselves. The Lord wants to use your genuine gifts and talents in the marketplace, in the church and at home. He desires that we demonstrate respect, honesty, kindness and faithfulness in a culture and a system that craves money, power and recognition. My husband, Charles, has often said to those who may be hungry for the spotlight, "There is only one Star and we killed Him." In other words, Jesus upheld the highest standard - the standard of perfection and the world hated Him for it. He is the one and only Star of the Ages. He is holy and we had the audacity to crucify Him. But praise God, He came back from the dead and nobody else has done that! Everything and everyone else pales in comparison to Him.

Here is the key to authenticity.

Raise the white flag. Surrender your gifts to God. He will elevate you to use your life as a godly example of what it looks like to have the blessings of God on your life. A life submitted to God does not make you weaker, but stronger. Colossians 3:23-24 reminds us, that it's not really an employer that we work for – but for Him. "Whatever you do, work heartily, as for the Lord and not for men, knowing that from the Lord you will receive the inheritance as your reward. You are serving the Lord Christ."

Raise the standard. Give God what's right, not what's left. In other words, give God your best. He wants you to raise the standard of excellence in a world that consistently does just enough to ease by. Don't pattern yourself after the world. You don't have the time or the energy for that mentality because that leads to nowhere. But you must raise the standard in everything you do, causing the world to see something in you that is real and desirable.

Raise your mindset. Are you ready and willing to step up in obedience to set the pace, never settling for mediocrity? Start by challenging yourself to think higher. Those with a worldly mindset will always want something for nothing. They will even fake it to try to make it. The truth, however, always exposes our motives.

As you think, so you will be. Elevate your thinking, expecting more of yourself. You will be the first to reap those benefits. You may think that challenge is too big for you. But it's not too big for God to work through you.

Just be yourself. Everyone else is already taken!

God has already qualified and equipped you with whatever it takes to make a difference in the world. The only requirement is, with the help of God, that you put the true, authentic, gifted, beautiful, anointed, powerful person you are, on display. You don't need the grace, the talent or the strength to be anyone else. God can't bless those who pretend to be something they're not. He can only bless who you really are. Just be yourself. Everyone else is already taken!

CALL TO ACTION

People are always observing you. If you give people something to talk about, let it be to your credit and for God's glory. Your life is constantly on display. Determine today that you will be your true, authentic self, so when others encounter you, they encounter Christ within you. Through your godly character people will be drawn to know Him more. Will you pray with me now?

Dear Father,

We are so humbled to be used by You! We want to have impeccable, Christ-like character and represent You well in everything we do. Help us to be true to You. Then we can be true to ourselves and our calling. There are times we have been selfish or even fearful, allowing our feelings, our vain desires, our greed and apprehensions to impede our progress. Forgive us where we fall short of all You want us to be. We will be mindful to use our opportunities, through our unique gifts and talents, to spread Your love so someone may see You in our lives.

In Jesus' name,

Amen

CHAPTER 2

BE YOUR BEST

"Behold, I have seen a son of Jesse the Bethlehemite, who is a skillful musician..."
1 Samuel 16:18

There is a great deal to be said about natural talent. You may have a natural propensity to sing, write songs, speak well, produce movies, play sports, dance, embrace technology, teach, possess leadership ability or excel in some other area. Natural talent is good. But natural talent is not enough. You must have skill. Have you ever noticed how people with skill make what they do look easy?

Have you observed Golden State Warrior guard, Stephen Curry's ability to shoot 3-pointers from all over the basketball court? New York Yankee, Derek Jeter, will go down in history for his performance as a champion in Major League Baseball. American music icon, Stevie Wonder is considered one of the most commercially successful musicians of our time. Captain Chesley Sullenberger is an American retired airline captain honored for the water landing of US Airways flight 1549 in the Hudson River after the aircraft was disabled when it struck a flock of geese. These people and people like them realize that natural ability can only take you so far. No doubt, they invested years of study, practice and application to arrive at a place where they would stand alone in their respective fields of expertise.

The definition of the word skill is defined as an ability and capacity acquired through deliberate, systematic, and sustained effort to smoothly and adaptively carry out complex activities or job functions involving ideas (cognitive skills), things (technical skills), and people (interpersonal skills). In simple terms, skill is the ability to do something with competence and excellence because of systematic practice over time and with discipline.

I find it interesting that the very first quality Saul's servant mentioned concerning David in 1 Samuel 16:18 was skill. Bible scholars suggest David wrote as many as 73 of the Psalms throughout his life. I'm sure David nurtured and developed those creative writing and music skills day after day while keeping his father's flocks. Imagine David spending hours and hours composing songs and playing the harp for an audience of dirty, smelly sheep. But David knew God was listening. Being his best for an Audience of One was David's main motivation. In due season, God would prepare the way to put David's gifts on display before an audience of many. You see, God always aligns passion with purpose. While David was tending the sheep, the need for his special talent was already developing. King Saul, a deeply troubled man, was an emotional and spiritual basket case. He failed to trust God time and time again and was often disobedient to God's instructions. Do you find that disobedience always opens the door to distress? Distress leads to a life that falls apart at the seams. Saul's very insightful servant saw the king's struggle and knew David's music was a remedy. What Saul's servant observed in David was a young man with an incredible set of skills that would meet a specific need. In essence, what the servant recognized was the ability to lead others into the presence of God! The word would spread. If you want to hear beautiful music that connects you with the heart of God, call David.

Isn't that what you want said about you? Do you desire to be the one others think of when a particular need arises? When someone needs an excellent musician to lead their congregation in songs of worship, do you want to come to mind? When an event coordinator needs a speaker for their conference, or a publisher needs a new author, wouldn't you like to be the one they call? When someone needs a graphic artist, a music producer, a costume designer, a choreographer, or whatever it is that you do, don't you wish they would call you? If your answer is yes, then you can be assured that the search will be on for someone with a high level of talent coupled with a unique skill set that separates the best from all the rest. To maximize your God-given potential as a creative person, endeavor to develop your gifts and talents consistently over time with hard work and discipline.

Ever since I was a young child, I was taught to work hard at developing my skills. Although I played for the church, my parents saw the raw musical potential I possessed and decided that I should take formal piano lessons. Immediately, I was thrown into the deep-end of music theory, learning to read music and play in every key. Soon after I assumed my responsibilities at the church, my gifts began to flourish as I rehearsed with choirs three nights a week and played all day every Sunday.

The choir members in our church did not read music. So, I had to learn to play the piano by ear at church while exercising my music reading skills when playing piano for choirs in junior high and high school. In high school, I began studying voice and continued my vocal music training on into college, then teaching in a middle high school classroom for almost eight years. All those years of music training gave me a good foundation for ministry and an edge that opened the door to many opportunities in my field of expertise.

There was a young, Black boy named Warren who grew up in the 1940's in the small farming community of Vacherie, Louisiana. While many of his relatives barely made ends meet working on cotton and sugarcane plantations, his parents were determined that Warren and his siblings would never work in the fields. One of ten children, Warren Dillon was raised by hard-working parents who instilled in him and his siblings, a relentless desire for hard work, a good education and excellence.

In fact, Warren and all of his siblings graduated from high school. Those who had the desire, went on to college, a tremendous feat for Black families at that time, in light of the fact that older children were most often needed at home to attend to the family farm. But Warren's family was different.

His mother was extremely business-minded and sold homemade sandwiches at a counter in a local store to help support their family, while his father worked in a factory making sheetrock. Dillon recalls that his father had so much pride and self respect that he never wore his work clothes to and from the factory, but wore rather nice street clothes to work instead. Then he would change into his work clothes once he arrived to work and back into his nice street clothes after his shift was over. Watching his parents' demonstrate pride in their accomplishments, a strong work ethic always impacted Dillon, who was taught never to be satisfied with average. Whenever he complained that something was too hard, his father's reply was always, "Son, you just haven't tried long enough." He was always an avid student, starting grade school early, graduating from high school and entering college at age 17.

Over the years Dillon and his siblings were taught that average was never good enough. There was an expectation at home and in the community that shaped his life as a young college student. While his other classmates were satisfied with getting a job, a car and an apartment, Warren desired to do much more with his life, despite any odds stacked against him. Later on, he would have responsibilities of marriage and raising a family, but he worked his way through college, earning his bachelor's, master's and doctoral degrees. He went on to work for more than two decades in the corporate world, using his math, science and technology skills. Today, Dr. Warren Dillon is the founder of In His Image Christian Academy outside of Atlanta, Georgia. For 20 years he has worked diligently to impact young people, challenging them to strive for excellence. He tells the young leaders

> *When you submit your natural talent and your skills to God, He will turn them into supernatural abilities every time."*
> *Dr. Warren Dillon*

under his tutelage, "The world is much bigger than your own environment. You may have natural talent, but your natural talent won't get you very far. You must have skill. When you submit your natural talent and your skills to God, He will turn them into supernatural abilities every time."

You see, if you really want to excel in your field of expertise, you'll need more than natural talent. You'll need to commit to hours of study and practice, spend hard-earned money, travel or whatever it takes. Please don't tell me you really want to be a scriptwriter, a recording artist, an actor, a fashion designer an author or anything creative, yet you've not performed your due diligence. L.A. Winters of A Thousand Word Pictures is an actor, producer and screenwriter. I met her 20 or so years ago when she worked as a drama director at her church. She has worked consistently over the years. Today she is realizing her dream as a producer of motion pictures. She knows what it means to invest years of hard work into her craft. L.A. Winters said this. "God put these dreams in my heart but I have recognized that they don't magically happen. I have invested time, money and attention to educating myself toward those dreams by stepping out in faith and taking classes on film-making, going to panel discussions and workshops, volunteering behind the camera, starting a monthly group of like-minded artists in my home, working with a screenwriting mentor and more. God gave me the dreams and continues to give me the inspiration to work toward them in His strength but with my actions. When I have felt inadequate or unqualified, God has reminded me that He doesn't call the qualified but He qualifies the called."

People tell me all the time of their desire to go into full-time music ministry and take their ministry on the road, yet, in many cases, they have done little to prepare themselves. A dear lady expressed to me, her desire to go into music ministry as a full-time vocation. I asked her to tell me about her music ministry experience. She told me she had two songs in her repertoire and two opportunities to sing in the last year. One song was sung at a wedding, the other at a funeral. Now, I'm not going to question the lady's calling, but with only two songs in her repertoire, and with only two appearances on her calendar in the last year, I simply advised her to really seek the Lord about full-time ministry as a vocation before she quit her day job!

A young writer gave me a copy of his movie script recently. He knew he fell short of the mark when I revealed to him there was no title page. His name and the title of his script were nowhere to be found. There was no contact information anywhere. The script even contained an abundance of misspelled words. If he had been given the fortunate opportunity to present his movie script to Steven Spielberg, the Kendrick Brothers, Oprah or some great Hollywood director, one glance and they would know this person could not be taken seriously. There's an accepted format to be followed. A standard of excellence has already been set by the industry. You must follow the format and always be aware of professional standards when presenting your work.

What I've learned is this. Leaning on natural talent alone will only limit your opportunities. You may have a lot of natural talent. But I assure you, if the person standing next to you has natural talent and skill, sooner or later they will move out ahead of you. They will enjoy more opportunity, touch more people and make more money because they worked harder at developing their skills and they know how to execute them. Let me tell a story that will drive my point home.

There were two sisters whose mother decided to enroll them into formal piano lessons. The older sister was a natural-born musician. She had a keen ear for music and she loved playing her own songs on the piano without any sheet music before her. The younger sister was not a natural musician but she practiced diligently on a daily basis. As the time for the annual recital drew near, their mother noticed the younger sister's discipline and how she practiced daily, methodically and consistently. As she practiced, her ability to play the piano consistently improved. The older sister, however, slacked off on practicing her assigned recital pieces. She spent her rehearsal time playing her own melodies at the piano, wasting away the time. Her mother reminded her regularly that the day of the recital was nearing. The older daughter bristled at her mother's rebuke assuring her mother that she would be ready for the performance. The day of the recital finally came. When it was time for the performance, the younger sister took the stage, sat at the piano and delivered her piano recital pieces flawlessly, receiving a standing ovation. The older sister, who had all the natural musical talent but applied no discipline, performed rather poorly. The child was embarrassed and ashamed of her pitiful performance, while her mother's heart ached as she looked on from the audience.

You see, gifts and talents are innate. You were born with them. Skill on the other hand, is developed through focus, drive and hard work. Skill is the difference-maker. Talent will take you to the lobby. Skill will take you inside to perform on the stage. Excellence will get you a return invitation. Embracing your natural talent is a great place to start. But to go the distance and find success, you'll need to invest time and energy studying your craft. Notice the word invest. This means you must spend time rehearsing, learning the desired skill, giving your audience your absolute best and improving your performance. You may need to spend money on books, classes, travel, transportation, clothing, and technical gear. By doing this, you will acquire the tools and techniques of the desired trade and you will be on your way to mastering them.

This is why coaching is so beneficial. My husband, Charles was a little league ball coach for more than three decades. He says, "Even a gifted player needs a coach because he has potential that needs to be developed. The most talented player still has potential he doesn't even know how to use". Your potential is not revealed all at once. You were never meant to reach a plateau and stay there. Over a lifetime, with knowledge, experience and opportunity, potential is discovered. We all need someone to show us the endless possibilities that exist inside of us. The most successful people I've coached are not those with the most talent, but those who recognize their untapped potential and are teachable. They are seekers. I know this personally, as well. Each time I have worked with a coach, I discover something new

"Even a gifted player needs a coach because he has potential that needs to be developed. The most talented player still has potential he doesn't even know how to use".
—Charles Mason

about myself and the gifts I possess. Learning on your own is fine. But learning with the assistance of a coach will help you to unearth the rich resources you already possess. A coach will help you see your potential from a different perspective with dimensions you may never see on your own. Besides, learning something new is fun! You may have graduated from school, but you must never quit learning.

Being satisfied with your own experience and settling for less, can prove very costly. Someone said ignorance is bliss. No, ignorance is expensive! Mistakes cost time, energy and money. So, be willing to learn from someone who has been where you are trying to go. And while I'm on the subject – before you consider investing hard-earned money into one of your own original projects, such as your own music recording, video or movie production, please get a professional to give you an honest assessment of your work. Seek the assistance of someone who does for a living, what you desire to do. They will help you to avoid costly mistakes, give you some guidance and help you decide whether you are ready to take the leap.

My very good friend and record producer, Cheryl Rogers is a great example of how skill can open doors for you. She has won four Emmy Awards and was the producer on the Grammy Award-winning Andrae Crouch Tribute project. Besides being an excellent songwriter and record producer, she has an array of gifts and talents, performing them all with impeccable ability. She has produced most of my recordings and arranged some of my most memorable songs, such as *With All My Heart, Each One Reach One, Trust His Heart, In All of His Glory, Shine The Light, Standing In The Gap, To The Cross, Play It Again, A World of Difference, Love Like That,* among a multitude of others. I've written songs in a number of genres from contemporary gospel, R&B, Jazz, Urban Gospel and songs that require lush, orchestral and choral arrangements. Cheryl masters each style with ease. I'm grateful to God for her because she understands my unique style. Listen to my music and you'll know what an outstanding musician she is.

Cheryl had this to say about skill. "I started playing the piano at age 5 and never looked back. God blessed me with talent, but if I never exercised that talent, learned more about it or just depended on what I had at age 5, I don't think I'd be doing music as a career. Talent has to be developed into

Talent has to be developed into skill and how much or how far you take your skill, sets you apart from others with similar talent. Skill is the result of taking talent to the finish line.
Cheryl Rogers

skill and how much or how far you take your skill, sets you apart from others with similar talent. Skill is the result of taking talent to the finish line. If you know you have talent in one area, you practice and learn everything you can in that area to perfect it. Learning to read music, playing the piano, singing, being in choirs, learning to arrange music, developing an ear for singing and playing in studio recording sessions, producing other musicians in the studio, etc. were the 'exercises' that helped me develop my talent into skill."

Most people spend more time working on their car than they spend working on their craft.

Cheryl Rogers and others like her have recognized their strengths, honed their craft and finely tuned their abilities. They have spent years working on their performance. As a result, they have played on the grandest stages the world over. They continue to embrace a work ethic that is incomparable. For them, average will never be good enough. These people do what the average person won't do. They consistently work on improving themselves and they never stop learning and making improvements. Ultimately, they stand in a class all by themselves and their services are in great demand. Day after day, they invest hours of sweat equity into their work and because of that, their phone keeps ringing. Most people spend more time working on their car than they spend working on their craft. Don't be that kind of person. If you want to rise above the average, then you must have an above average work ethic.

If you're not progressing you're digressing. Those who are fully qualified in the 21st century are strategically moving forward. They are prepared when their moment arrives and they never make excuses or use disclaimers. They don't let things like age, race, income or even a common cold put constraints on them. Every fully qualified person knows that some days things just happen organically. Other days, those who have mastered their skills know they must eventually put feet to their prayers and make things happen no matter what. Good things always happen for those who work hard. Opportunity just seems to find them.

I'll never forget the time skill saved my day. I had been invited to sing for a conference on leadership. The conference host informed me that I was to sing one song after the keynote speaker. There was no need to speak or introduce the song – just step out onto the stage and sing. No problem. I could do that! The subject of the speaker's message was Keeping It Together When Life Falls Apart. After the message, I stepped out on stage. The music soundtrack started and I sang through the first verse. As the song flowed into the first chorus, the soundtrack stopped. I was living a singer's worst nightmare. Dead, cold silence - before an audience of 1,500 people! When I asked the sound guys to roll the track again, they looked back with a quizzical stare and hunched their shoulders. There was a piano on stage. So, I said to the audience, "No problem. I'll just go over here to the piano and play the song from there." What I hadn't told them was that I hadn't played the song from the piano since the day the song was recorded several years prior. I had been using the music soundtrack in my performances! Thank God for that extra edge. Thank God for all those years of playing the piano by ear in my father's church. If I hadn't developed that skill, I don't what I would have done. I sat at the piano and played a four bar intro on the fly and sang the first verse. As I started into the chorus the room erupted into applause. I sang the second verse. When I got to the second chorus, they applauded again. I sang the bridge of the song, modulated to a new key and laid into the last chorus with conviction, finishing on a high note. The audience rose to their feet in a thunderous ovation! At that moment, I realized I had just become the object lesson for the speaker's keynote address. After the session, people came by my product table in the lobby to comment and even compliment me on how the situation was handled. I even sold out of all the books and CD's I had brought. I learned something that day. You cannot predict the outcome of every performance. So you must be prepared for any number of things that could happen. Most people have some kind of talent. What separates the talented from the successful is hours and hours of hard work that will prepare you for skillful performance.

Here's something to remember.

Take off the limits. Natural talent alone will only take you so far. What you may lack in natural talent can be fully realized when coupled with skill and discipline. If you want to succeed in life, go the extra mile. While others may do just enough to get by, you must go beyond what is expected. Discipline yourself to become a skillful person. Learn your craft inside and out. Never rest on what you've accomplished in the past or be satisfied with doing less. If you do that, you'll become addicted to mediocrity. You must never let that happen. Excellence is timeless and never goes out of style. Perfection may not be possible, but when perfection is diligently pursued, excellence will always be the end result.

> *Never rest on what you've accomplished in the past or be satisfied with doing less. If you do that, you'll become addicted to mediocrity.*

Take your time. Enjoy the journey. It seems the world we are living in tends to be moving faster and faster. Emails, text messages and social media all seem to pressure us to respond immediately, while we tend to be more distracted, spending less and less time engaging with people. You don't have to succumb to the harried and hurried way the world is going. Hurry is the enemy of excellence. When you sit down to read, pray or brainstorm, turn your phone on silence to avoid unnecessary distractions. Beeps, chirps and chimes are sure to be groove-busters when you need to be creative. Next, take your time with people. Look people in the eye and engage their presence when you are in conversations. It's not only good etiquette, it's emotionally validating to give people 100% of your time and all of your attention. While it's important to master technology and stay current on the latest trends, connecting with people is far more important. Then take your time when you are working on your projects. When you hurry through a project, you're more likely to miss important details and we all know that it's the little things that mean a lot. Be methodical, checking and double-checking your work. No matter how good you are, (or how good you think you are) mistakes are always more likely to occur when you are in a hurry.

Take your skill up a notch – Learning to play a musical instrument or develop some other skill? You'll get better faster if you apply what you are learning to real-life situations. Place a demand on your skill by pushing yourself toward a LIVE performance goal. Don't think you're ready to take your performance to the stage? It may be time to give yourself a needed push. Once, while crossing a busy street, a motorcycle came speeding from around a blind curve, heading straight for me. Immediately, I shifted into high gear, sprinting across the busy street at a fast clip. My left knee is challenged from an old injury. But that didn't seem to slow me down. I was running so fast, I had to break my speed once I arrived to the other side. I was amazed at how agile I was and even said to myself, "Wow, I didn't know I had all that in me!" That is what potential looks like! You have more in you than you realize. Place a demand on your potential. You'll be surprised at what you can accomplish.

Take action. Don't fall prey to the myth that once you achieve a certain level of ability you can rest there. You have talents even now that are lying dormant. You might say, "I'm good enough." But good enough is never good enough. High achieving, ministry-minded believers are always willing to push forward, exploring new territory. Stretch yourself. Do you need to embrace technology, complete a project or explore new ways to grow your audience? Don't be intimidated on one hand or lulled into a false sense of security on the other hand. Stay current with the world around you by opening your mind to new experiences. Read a book or take a course. Get involved in my mentoring and coaching program and fine tune your skills to help you keep that competitive edge. Attend my weekend LIVE events for singers, songwriters and self-published authors called The Inner Circle. Promote your music or your book on my internet radio station, Babbie Mason Radio(www.babbiemasonradio.com). Any of these events will help to give you information, motivation and an edge that separates you from the average.

Take a risk. When I was a young songwriter all of my songs sounded good to me. However, when I became a more serious songwriter, I started attending songwriting workshops and forums where I could get feedback on my writing. I realized I had much to learn. In my hometown I was a big fish in a little pond. But when my songs were displayed on a national stage, I learned quickly that I was a little fish in a big pond and there was room for much improvement. I took the risk and put my work out there on the public stage where people could hear it. One big lesson I learned was that honest assessment of my work was necessary for my advancement. I also learned quickly that constructive criticism of my work was not an attack on me as a person. You must understand that. If you want to be better at your craft, let go of your super sensitive feelings. This can be a difficult, painful process. Becoming attached to your work can be so easy to do. Be careful not to become blind to your imperfections and resistant to change. If you want to improve, you must hold your work loosely and embrace constructive criticism. You'll find receiving this form of teaching from a professional only makes you better.

I remember once, during a songwriting competition I attended years ago, a young songwriter's composition was being critiqued by a panel of professional writers and publishers. The panel had some very harsh but honest criticisms of the song and suggested that the composer do a rewrite. The young, inexperienced songwriter said in defense of his song, "I can't change the song. God gave me this song!" One professional publisher replied, "No, God did not give you this song. God writes better than this!" Remember, if you want to get better at anything, embrace feedback and learn to let go.

Take It Online – This may sound harsh, but there is truth to what I heard someone say recently, "Concerning ministry and business, if you don't have some kind of presence on the internet, you'll soon become irrelevant." This doesn't speak to the quality of your talent, but to the potential of your impact. The whole world is online. If you want to reach the world and impact people with your message, to stay relevant in this fast-paced world, you must keep up with technology. Connecting with people online may intimidate you. But you can do it. Start with small steps as you learn to navigate the internet and connect with others online. Keep your message consistent and be open to reinvention. What worked for you a few years ago may not be what works for you now. Over the course of my career, I have recorded music on 8-track tape, albums and 45's, cassettes, CD's and digital downloads! Today, the compact disk player is becoming obsolete. Some automobile manufacturers are not putting CD players in their cars anymore.

I've had to come to grips with these changes then reinvent and reevaluate how I write, record, promote and sell my music. It will be necessary to assess your goals and strategies often to assure that your current plan is working for you. You may decide to take a class on social media, become more proficient in your computer skills, learn to play an instrument, learn a foreign language or attend a conference or workshop in your desired field of expertise. Keep moving! You'll never get where you're going by lamenting over the way things used to be.

God didn't overlook you when He was passing out gifts. God sent you. God meant you! He has given everyone a plethora of gifts – including you! Don't worry about being qualified. Because of Jesus you are already fully qualified for your assignment and you already have God's stamp of approval on your life. You are called. You are capable and you already have the capacity to receive more. The potential is already in you. But you must maximize that potential.

Take the gifts and talents God gave you and do something with them. You're not competing with anyone but yourself. The Apostle Paul says this in 1 Corinthians 7:7 "I wish that all men were as I am. But each man has his own gift from God; one has this gift, another has that." Your gifts and talents, which are many, are given to you by God. They are a unique fit for you.

Prepare yourself, because right now, somewhere in the world, your services are needed. Your gift is a lifeline to someone. Remember this. Duty is yours. The results are the Lord's. In other words, excel in your giftedness and be ready when your moment comes.

CALL TO ACTION

A few years ago I was invited to fly to another city to sing in a concert when another Christian singer got sick at the last minute. My schedule permitted, so I packed my bag, flew to the city and did the concert.

If your phone rang right now and the person on the other end of phone invited you, right this very minute, to fulfill the opportunity you've only dreamed about, would you be ready? Ask God to reveal your passions, those things that really move you or burden your heart. That information is not a secret. He wants to reveal His plans to you more than you want to know them. What changes do you need to make to get ready for your moment? Many people will not take the necessary time to improve themselves. But hopefully you know to take all the time you need to prepare then be quick to seize the next opportunity. You owe it to yourself to make strategic plans that will move you forward. When most people are settling for less, you must determine to be your best and get what you want out of life.

Allow me to pray for you that you would approach and complete every assignment with skill and excellence.

Dear Heavenly Father,

Thank You for blessing us with many opportunities to bring glory to Your name. We want to be skillful, hard-working and disciplined. Nothing less than our best will do. Forgive us when we have had an attitude of entitlement or missed an opportunity because we were unprepared. We dedicate our gifts and talents to You all over again. You gave us these gifts for a reason and that is to make Your name famous. So today, we'll hone our skills, go into our world and make You look good!

In Jesus' name,

Amen

CHAPTER 3

BE BRAVE

"Behold, I have seen a son of Jesse the Bethlehemite who is a skillful musician, a mighty man of valor...." 1 Samuel 16:18

One day a man went to the woods to hunt bear. He hunted an entire day without seeing one bear. Finally, at the end of the day he decided to call it quits. He put his rifle back into his truck and went for a walk down by the river. He wasn't on his walk five minutes when he saw a big black bear charging straight for him. Immediately, the man shouted, "Please God! Make this bear a Christian bear!" All of a sudden the bear stopped in his tracks, folded his hands in prayer and said, "Dear Lord, thank You for this food I'm now about to receive."

You probably won't be encountering big, hungry bears any time soon. But to navigate life with all of its challenges and demands, you need huge doses of courage for those situations that cause you fear and distress. If you want to do anything for God, anything at all, fear will always be a factor. But don't be intimidated or let fear talk you out of all God has in store for you.

Valor is a word that may not be used a great deal in our modern day vocabulary, but it is a great personal quality. Valor is defined as possessing great courage in the face of danger, especially in battle. Men and women of war from centuries past have possessed raw courage, bravery, and fearlessness when facing their enemies on the battlefield. What about you? Do you consider yourself a man or woman of valor, possessing those inner qualities of deep courage to stand toe to toe and face your enemies? Fear may prevent you from singing your song or speaking from the stage. You may experience suffocating anxiety even at the thought of getting on an airplane. Whatever it is that causes you to panic, you can overcome it with the help of the Lord. His Word says in Romans 8:31, "If God be for us, who can be against us?"

When God is on your side you can come out of your corner and face your threats like a bold warrior. Those who are the least likely are the ones God is looking for. If you are fearful, you are not alone. Popular Christian author, Max Lucado said this. "The presence of fear does not mean you have no faith. Fear visits everyone. But make your fear a visitor and not a resident." God, on the inside of you is greater than any outward enemy you may face. He'll fight your battle so you will come out a victor every time, regardless of how big your enemy appears to be. To maximize your God-given potential, call on your inner courage with stalwart strength and

> *"The presence of fear does not mean you have no faith. Fear visits everyone. But make your fear a visitor and not a resident."*
> *Max Lucado*

deep conviction.

David was that kind of young man. While he was keeping his father's sheep, no doubt he found himself in situations where he had to take risks, operating with courage and confidence in the face of danger. Protecting his father's flocks at all cost, David had to defend the helpless animals from wild beasts, thieves, inclement weather and anything that would do them harm. And we all know the story of how David slew Goliath.

King Saul was a tall man, at least a head taller than any other Israelite (1 Samuel 9:2). Yet, when Goliath came out to confront the king and his armies, Saul was terrified. (1 Samuel 17:11) Everyone else was terrified too; except for David. He assured the king he would take care of the threatening bully. You know the rest of the story. David was a brave and fearless young man. He had great confidence in his heart because he had great confidence in His God. While some thought the giant was too big to hit, David believed the giant was too big to miss. With a sling and a stone, David aimed for the 9 foot terror and nailed him right between the eyes. Like a timbering tree, Goliath, the Philistine fell dead! That's the kind of courage we need – courage to look our threats in the eye, call on the God we know is on our side and fight back!

Can you imagine performing musical selections on demand? David was kind of like a human iTunes playlist. Knowing that the king was prone to severe mood swings and fits of rage, one false move, one flat note or one poor song choice and the king could have ordered David's execution. This was an indication of Saul's weakness. He was narcissistic, self-absorbed and self-conscious. But, David's confidence and calling were not in his own abilities. His confidence was in the Lord. He knew wherever the Lord guided him, the Lord would provide for him.

Jon Acuff, a renowned speaker and author hired by financial

guru, Dave Ramsey, says basically, that fear is the thing that prevents most people from fulfilling their potential. We all have hopes, dreams, passions and desires, but a lot of us give in to fear as soon as we get close to fulfilling them. "The reason is that fear only gets loud when you do things that matter. Fear never bothers you if you're average, but the second you dare to be more than ordinary, fear awakens."

"The reason is that fear only gets loud when you do things that matter. Fear never bothers you if you're average, but the second you dare to be more than ordinary, fear awakens."
Jon Acuff

That's profound! That's how you know you are on the right track! Don't give in to fear when you feel the heat of it breathing down your neck. When you've got too much month and not enough money, giving up is not an option. If you've been thinking about going back to school and getting your college degree, don't let the naysayers talk you out of it. You know as well as I do - whenever you want to do anything that makes a difference, you will always have to fight for it. Famous author and lecturer, Dale Carnegie, knew this all too well. He grew up a poor farm boy but always had a love for persuasive speech. As a young salesman, he excelled at his job, selling bacon, soap and lard for a meat packing company. Carnegie experienced numerous failed attempts at business before writing his most popular work, "How To Win Friends and Influence People", which sold millions of copies in multiple languages. He knew personally, the only way to fight fear is to face it. He said, "If you want to conquer fear, don't sit at home and think about it. Go out and get busy." God wants to take you from where you are to the next chapter of your life story. Just as God did for David in Bible times and contemporary successful business people, God will provide the courage and fearlessness you need. But it won't happen until you look your giant in the face and say, "Okay giant! In the name of Jesus, you have to fall."

It took a great deal of courage to quit my job as a middle school music teacher back in 1984. My husband, Charles had started a new business back then. Although his business was growing, we depended on my paycheck and the health care benefits that came with working as a teacher for the state of Georgia. We had a growing family and the benefits package was a nice safety net. As more and more opportunities to sing began to come my way, that budding dream to become a singer began to interfere with my day job. The day came when I had to submit the Intent To Return form on a Tuesday morning in early spring of that year, letting the county know if I would return to teach the following fall. I wanted to start my singing career but common sense slammed the brakes on my dream. The Monday night before the form was due, my friend Barb came by the house with an evangelist friend of hers and his wife. Barb wanted us to meet in hopes that this would open a door for me to sing in his evangelistic meetings. We chatted for about an hour. I even sang a couple of songs at the big grand piano that sat in our small living room. As evening set in, Barb, the evangelist and his wife rose to leave. It was then the evangelist asked me if I had any prayer needs. I told him of my deep desire to quit my job and step out in faith but the fact that we wouldn't be able to afford health insurance was a deep concern. I told him of the Intent To Return form that was due the next morning. We all prayed. What happened next was a miracle. The evangelist, whom I had just met, said he felt impressed to buy our health insurance for the first year of ministry so I could quit my job! I checked 'no' on the form and turned the form in the next morning. I finished the year out and never looked back.

God's hand of favor has been preparing the way for this ministry from the start. Down through the years I've recorded ten music projects on my own and fifteen recordings for major record labels, written books for well-known publishers, sung on stages at Carnegie Hall, Billy Graham Crusades, The Grammy Awards and Bill Gaither's Homecoming events. I've performed with Quincy Jones, Gladys Knight, Peabo Bryson and Al Jarreau on the Handel's Soulful Messiah recording, stood before American presidents, Carter, Ford and Bush, toured with Women of Faith and The Young Messiah Tour. I've ministered in thousands of churches of various sizes, denominations and cultures, worked with national and international ministries such as Youth For Christ, the Navigators, Youth With A Mission, Trans World Radio, Focus on The Family, Operation Mobilization, TBN, Atlanta's WATC-TV 57, The 700 Club, 100 Huntley Street, Dr. Charles Stanley's In Touch, Beth Moore, Kay Arthur and countless radio and television programs – all without a booking agent or professional management team.

Again, I am by no means boasting about all of this. I know I'm not the best performer there is. There are others who write better songs than I do. But, one thing is true. I have never been afraid of hard work. Hard work

God doesn't call those who are able as much as He calls those who are available.

reaps great dividends. God doesn't call those who are able as much as He calls those who are available. Success rarely comes to those who only wish for it. But success is much more likely to present one opportunity after another to those who work for it.

Nysi Kilgore knows what it means to yield herself to God in spite of any apprehension. She began her studies to be ordained as a minister at age 13 and was ordained at age 16. She launched two businesses as a teenager. She was valedictorian of her graduating class. She has graduated from college and is working on her master's degree. She has written her first book, God Is: Lessons I Learned About God In College. The remarkable thing is, Nysi is only 20 years old. She has a phenomenal family that supports her in all her endeavors. In spite of all that, there were times when Nysi faced insurmountable challenges as she tried to live up to the expectations of others. Nysi was a guest on my TV show, Babbie's House and I asked her to give hope to those who are struggling with inner doubts and fears. She said, "Your past does not disqualify you. God loves using broken things. You can use your brokenness as a platform for your calling and your future. Regardless of who supports you or not, everything you need to accomplish your calling is on the inside of you. You are more than capable. You are unstoppable. Even if fear creeps up on the inside of you, do it afraid."

> *You are more than capable. You are unstoppable. Even if fear creeps up on the inside of you, do it afraid."*
> *Nysi Kilgore*

Nysi Kilgore's words resonate deeply with me. Sometimes you have to 'do it afraid'. I have been getting on and off airplanes for as long as I have been in ministry. I've logged over two million miles and counting with one airline. But, right after September 11, 2001, when all those planes crashed and took so many lives, I became tremendously afraid to fly. The very thought of getting on an airplane caused me to panic, break out in cold sweats and hyperventilate. I shared what I was going through with a friend and she said something I'll never forget. She said, "Babbie, the enemy has targeted you to fill your heart with fear." When she said the words 'targeted you', I got a mental picture of a bull's-eye plastered across my back. Then I envisioned the devil aiming at me, shooting his fiery darts of fear, anxiety and panic at me. At that very moment my whole being riled up with righteous indignation. I remember saying out loud, "Oh no devil! I will not be a tormented by you! Target practice ends now!"

I knew I had a flight to catch exactly one week from that day. Immediately, I immersed myself in God's Word and began to memorize as many scriptures as I could that related to overcoming fear, gaining courage and God's power on the inside of me. One of the passages that gave me tremendous comfort was Psalm 91. The passage begins, "He that dwelleth in the secret place of the Most High shall abide under the shadow of the Almighty." The day of my flight came. I wish I could say that the fear had left me. It hadn't. But I was confident that I was on a mission and God would take care of me. Before putting my carry-on bag into the overhead compartment, I reached into the side pocket for my Bible. The version I usually carry was missing! The Bible that I always carry with me, the one with the well-worn cover - the copy that I have underlined, highlighted in yellow and written my name in the margins of my favorite passages – was gone. But there in the same place was a copy of the Message Bible. I don't remember how it got there but I retrieved it from the side pocket, sat down in my seat, buckled myself in and began to read Psalm 91.

> You who sit down in the High God's presence,
>
> spend the night in Shaddai's shadow,

Say this: "GOD, you're my refuge.

I trust in you and I'm safe!"

That's right—he rescues you from hidden traps,

shields you from deadly hazards.

His huge outstretched arms protect you—

under them you're perfectly safe;

I continued to read the whole chapter over and over again. Then I leaned my head back into the headrest to pray. Not long after that I was awakened by the flight attendant asking me if I wanted peanuts or pretzels! I know for myself that God will give you the peace which surpasses all understanding that will guard your heart and mind in Christ Jesus, according to Philippians 4:7. That experience taught me a life lesson: Winning the battle doesn't require physical strength. It requires trust in the Lord. When life presses in on all sides and the storm rages within, that's the time to stop looking at the circumstances around you and call on God's Word within you! If you are a victim of this kind of fear, God can and will enable you to be victorious. Remember 2 Timothy 1:7. "For God has not given us the spirit of fear. But of power, and of love and of a sound mind." KJV

You can overcome fear on or off the stage with preparation. When I am learning a new song or developing a new message I want to speak to my audiences, I do much more than just memorize words. I prepare mentally, meditating on the message or the song countless times so I know the material from memory, inside and out. I involve my facial expressions as I say or sing certain words. I make hand movements and gestures in dedicated places. I memorize vocal inflections in particular phrases. I practice stage presence and body language to help with memory retention and delivery. Spiritually, I spend time in prayer so I can be at my best and minister to the numerous needs of people. I prepare physically, warming up my voice before each performance. I avoid caffeine, dairy products, chocolate, and anything that will prohibit me from performing at my absolute best. I am extremely conscious not to overwork or strain my voice. I know my vocal limits and I operate freely within those boundaries. I really do want to sing all of my life, so I don't shout, scream or abuse my voice. I rehearse so I'll remember. And I prepare so I will not soon forget. When I've done all this, I know I'm ready to step out on the center stage and lift my voice, with confidence to the glory of God.

I do know the feeling of that last minute adrenaline rush I sometimes experience before going on stage. Some people call that feeling 'butterflies' in the pit of your stomach or last minute nerves. But I welcome that sensation! I define that nervous energy as anticipation. All that energy reminds me, too, that after all my preparation, I'm still deeply and humanly fallible. Leaning on my own strength is the perfect set-up for failure. If I want to keep my message relevant, my heart right, my head clear and my performance fresh then I'd better be dependent on the Lord's anointing to help me accomplish what I've been sent to do! Although I've been on stage thousands of times, I always pray and ask God to enable me to do what He has called me to do for that particular occasion.

What's your take-away from all of this? The call on your life is bigger than you can accomplish on your own. That assignment can be intimidating. You're going to need courage from the Lord to get it done. One public speaker was so nervous when it came time for her to speak, the audience could hear her heart pounding through her lapel microphone. When it comes time for you to step out you might be shaking in your shoes, but if you're not attempting something that gives you cause for pause, your dream is probably too small. You can choose to walk in fear and be a prisoner of panic or you can walk in faith and be an overcomer! Realize God has already equipped you for the task. Memorize 1 John 4:4. "Ye are of God, little children, and have overcome them: because greater is he that is in you, than he that is in the world." Don't be fooled into thinking that valor is a quality only for men. Regardless of your race, color, church affiliation or gender, you must see yourself as God sees you. Don't label yourself something you'll have to be delivered from later. You are not weak, a victim or a hopeless case. You are already empowered, enabled and endowed for the task before you. Here are more suggestions to fill your heart with courage:

Say hello to purpose. God has a specific mission and a strategic plan He wants to fulfill through you. He has some blessings with your name on them. If you haven't already done so, pray and ask the Lord to reveal His plan and purpose for your life. By faith, step out in obedience. Even small steps are a big deal to God. There may be others who may have a similar call or assignment. That's okay. Don't let that deter or distract you. No one can do what you can do exactly like you can do it.

Say goodbye to procrastination. On a regular basis, mentally, spiritually and physically take inventory of your skill set to determine areas where you may need to improve. Maybe you've said, "I really would like to write a book." Or "I need to lose weight." Don't put off any longer, the things you consider important. Opportunity has a window. Open the window and seize your moment.

All you need is the want to. God will give you the will to.

Procrastination is the thief of time. Really, procrastination is disobedience in slow motion.

If you are a procrastinator, ask yourself why you continue to put things off. Are you afraid of what the outcome might be? Are you fearful of the process? Do you dread the work involved? Remember, most of the things we fear never become reality. Ask God for His help. All you need is the want to. God will give you the will to. No doubt, you could come up with a million and one excuses not to make the necessary improvements, such as not having enough time, you're short on finances or there's no one to encourage you. Determine to live in an excuse-free zone. Results will come when you stop making excuses and start making changes. As the Lord sees your faithfulness, even in small things, He will reward you.

Set your pace. Have the courage to live your own life! You are the CEO of your own story. Focus on your ministry and business path. Don't be distracted by what or how someone else is doing their thing. If someone you know is moving in a different direction, cheer them on!

By the way, my husband, Charles offers some great advice. He has often said, "Don't go into full-time ministry until your ministry is taking up your full-time." Charles warns against quitting your job to sit at home to wait for the phone to ring. You have options now. The internet is the new frontier. Launching your business or ministry online can give you opportunity to plan your next steps and start a business without leaving home or quitting your job. And when it's time to take the next leap, you'll know it.

Have the courage to jump in with both feet and make a splash! Too many people are content but they're not fulfilled. They play it safe. Just because you're used to a place doesn't mean you have to stay there. Step by step, start moving forward toward your goal and God will give you the road map with necessary directions at your own pace and at just the right time.

Shine your light. Matthew 5:16 says, "Let your light so shine before men that they may see your good works and glorify your Father who is in heaven." In other words, the only way to be a light is to turn it on in the midst of darkness.

When you are a witness for God, you are always on display. You represent Christ wherever you go, not just when you are on stage. Pray that God will give you clear and concise words to speak for Him with boldness, compelling people to follow Christ – on stage or off. Unfortunately, you may not always be able to speak about Jesus in some places such as on your job or other public places. Regardless, people will observe your behavior.

Others will listen to your conversations. Do you honor your word? Do you value other people's time? Are you kind to people and treat them with respect? People are listening to what you say, and they are observing the things you do. Preach the gospel everywhere you go. Use words when necessary.

Simple is best. Sometimes we overcomplicate things. Shooting for the moon is a lofty goal, but sometimes we aim so high we become overwhelmed by our dream. The next thing we know, we have stopped before we can get started.

Simplicity is one of the greatest assets a dreamer can have. Here is some advice. Start with the one thing you do really well, then master that one thing before adding another skill. The most successful businesses we know are well known for a reason: They focus on being the best at one thing.

CALL TO ACTION

Today is a day to go where you have never gone before. It's time to do what you have never done before. You have your marching orders. Now get started. Don't let fear stop you, no matter what. Fear is only a distraction to keep you from accomplishing your assignment. I once saw this acronym for FEAR: False Evidence Appearing Real. God is fighting for you and you have already overcome. Remember this passage. Even set it to memory. Joshua 1:9.

> "Have not I commanded thee? Be strong and of a good
> courage; be not afraid, neither be thou dismayed: for the
> LORD thy God is with thee whithersoever thou goest."

It's time to pray. Let's ask God for the spirit of boldness. We're going to need it for the journey ahead.

> Sweet Father,
>
> Thank You for the strength and confidence we find in Your Word. We wouldn't even be able to put one foot in front of the other without your strength. With Your power working in us, Your presence all around us and all of heaven pulling for us, there is no way we can lose. And in those moments when our knees knock together and fear knocks at our heart's door, we will claim the courage You alone can give, step out in the spotlight - even when we are afraid - and do our thing for You!
>
> In Jesus' name,
>
> Amen

CHAPTER 4

BE AN ENCOURAGER

Behold, I have seen a son of Jesse the Bethlehemite who is a skillful musician, a mighty man of valor, a warrior, one prudent in speech...
l Samuel 16:18

Have you ever offered someone an encouraging word and found how quickly their outlook changed? Without encouraging words, we would often be overwhelmed by very real situations we all face. That is what I hope to accomplish through this book – to offer words of wisdom from my own experiences to encourage and guide you. That's what I believe David did for his young counterparts.

Even as a young man, David knew the power of encouraging words. He recognized that words have the power to build people up or tear people down, to heal or to injure, to bring life or to cause death. Somewhere along the line, David may have offered a word of advice or an encouraging word to Saul's servant. Uplifting words and acts of kindness are not easily forgotten. When the young servant was before the king, he described David's words as prudent, which means practical, sensible, wise and pragmatic. David was young but he was anointed by God to speak a ready word for the right moment. Saul was an emotionally unstable man. God sent David to his residence to minister to Saul with words and music that sent Saul's inner demons on the run.

Words have power and life! Words that build people up can be like medicine to the soul. Proverbs 16:24 says. "Pleasant words are like a honeycomb, sweetness to the soul and health to the bones." In a day and age where people are always ready to cut others down with hurtful words, you must be mindful to build people up with words that edify and encourage. To maximize your God-given potential as a communicator, exercise the use of encouraging words and deeds to benefit others.

I know what it's like to be down and discouraged and need an encouraging word. Just after I left the teaching profession in 1984, my dear friend and songwriting buddy, Donna Douglas Walchle told me about a music conference in Estes Park, Colorado called the Christian Artist Music Seminar in The Rockies. Donna and my husband, Charles encouraged me to go. Donna purchased a plane ticket but Charles and I had limited funds so we had no choice but to drive. We believed it was God who supplied our needs when a few days prior to our trip, a Shell Gas credit card came in the mail. We didn't know it at the time, but there were no Shell Gas Stations west of St. Louis! We arrived in Estes Park, Colorado two days later, exhausted from the drive, low on cash, but excited about the conference that drew anybody who was anybody - musicians, singers, songwriters, record company executives and music publishers. We ate peanut butter sandwiches and bologna and crackers all week to assure we had enough gas money to get back home to Georgia. That week would prove to be the week that changed my life.

People from all over the globe came to this seminar nestled high in the Rocky Mountains of Colorado. The competition was fierce, but I thought I had a shot. I had entered one of my compositions in the songwriting competition, Called We've Got A Reason To Celebrate. I thought my song was the best thing that had happened to the world since sliced bread.

> *My songs are like spiritual children to me. It was like those songwriting judges had told me my baby was ugly.*

The competition adjudicators didn't think so. They said the lyrics were trite and full of Christian-ese. That's a predictable language that only Christians speak. They said the melody was commonplace and boring. My songs are like spiritual children to me. It was like those songwriting judges had told me my baby was ugly. My song would not be advancing to the finals. I was hurt and disappointed. My dreams were dashed. We had spent a lot of money to get out there and it was looking like it was all for naught.

That week I sat in on a songwriting workshop and I also entered the vocal competition. By the end of the conference I had advanced to the winner's circle and won Third Place in the Vocal Competition! I was excited about all I had learned and experienced. With my shiny new 3rd Place trophy in tow, I was all excited about my win until the enemy began to whisper in my ear on the long ride home. "You're a no-good songwriter and a last-place singer. You'll never make it. And oh yeah, by the way, you just quit your day job!" I tried to pray my way through my bouts with discouragement. I began second-guessing all the decisions I had made in the recent weeks. One day, not long after arriving home from the conference, I was inspired by a song idea. I envisioned standing before the Throne in heaven with every nation, tribe, people and language (Revelation 7:9-12). A few minutes later I had written a song called, All Rise. The chorus says:

With my shiny new 3rd Place trophy in tow, I was all excited about my win until the enemy began to whisper in my ear on the long ride home.

> *All rise! All rise!*
>
> *We stand before the throne*
>
> *In the presence of the Holy One*
>
> *All rise! All rise!*
>
> *As we worship the Messiah*
>
> *All rise!*

I showed the song to the music minister at my church. He gave me the encouragement I needed. He even had the song arranged by our orchestra director so our church choir could sing it. All Rise is now a signature song I have sung in just about every concert since the day I wrote it. It's been recorded and arranged hundreds of times.

By the way, we went back to the Christian Artist Music Seminar in Estes Park, Colorado the following year, in 1985. I entered All Rise into the songwriting competition. Award-winning singer/songwriter, Scott Wesley Brown was one of the adjudicators, along with a host of other distinguished critics. All the judges gave the song high marks.

Later that week, All Rise would win the First Place Prize for the winning song. I would win the First Place Prize in the Vocal Competition, too. And a few years later Scott Wesley Brown would record All Rise on one of his recordings.

I've tasted discouragement over the years, as I have stood by the grave of both of my parents. I have sat by the hospital bed of my husband while he was in intensive care after suffering a stroke. Donna Douglas Walchle has won all kinds of awards for her songwriting, including seven Platinum Records for a song she wrote called, The Hard Way, recorded by Country Music legend, Faith Hill. However, she knows what it's like to receive discouraging news after a cancer diagnosis – not once but four times. God is turning things around in her favor as we speak. This is what she told me to tell you.

"We're always being prepared for a prize. We have to be faithful to go through the training period. If you look at Babbie's and my 30 plus years as friends, it's been about preparation for the prize. No matter what we're facing, we can know one thing for certain; good will come of this and our prize is coming. We may not see it and we may not understand it. But this is God's promise. One

"When I stand before God at the end of my life I hope I would not have a single bit of talent left, but could say, I used everything You gave me."
Comedian, Erma Bombeck

word from Him and our storm is quieted. One touch from Him and our problem is resolved. He's got you in the palm of His hand, so start praising Him for His faithfulness."

For over three decades, my husband Charles and I have been hosting workshops and conferences because we have always felt God's call to pour into the lives of independent singers, songwriters and self-published authors. As a matter of fact, I'm trying to get as much of my knowledge and experiences out of me while I can. I love what Comedian Erma Bombeck said, "When I stand before God at the end of my life I hope I would not have a single bit of talent left, but could say, I used everything You gave me." With all of my heart, that's my story, too!

Maybe you are discouraged or frustrated because you're not making the progress you had hope to make by now. That's why I wrote this book; to help you stay encouraged. I've experienced first-hand what it's like to be discouraged. But just like our experience at Estes Park, you have to take the good with the bad and learn from every situation you face.

God's Word promises that even your worst situation can work out for your good. Keep moving in the right direction. Believe what Donna said, that good will come of whatever it is you're going through. Be open to new experiences. In spite of disappointment, you must get up and try again. You may even have to unlearn some bad habits and replace those with new practices. But you can do it because you are an extraordinary person. You see, an ordinary person wouldn't even take time to read this book. Small-minded thinkers make excuses when they fail. They take short-cuts, hoping to get something for nothing. Big thinkers like you take responsibility for their successes. They know that taking the high road might be the long way around but it's on the high road where you will find few distractions, the best views and uncharted territory.

Here are some more ways you can build your confidence as a communicator and encourage people whether you are in business or in ministry.

Be good to people. Being genuinely good to people is perhaps, the most important thing you can do to advance your ministry and career. Continually cultivate the desire to be a people-builder, always showing people that you care. Ever heard the phrase kindness is contagious? That's very true! If you believe in people, doing all you can to edify them, good things will come back to you. Remember this short proverb:

If you want happiness for an hour – take a nap.

If you want happiness for a day – go fishing.

If you want happiness for a month - take a vacation.

If you want happiness for a year - inherit a fortune.

If you want happiness for a lifetime – be good to others.

Believe in your story. Audiences appreciate information but they lean in and listen to stories. When told well, a great story can engage your audience and become a key to a compelling presentation, inspiring and motivating your audience. Storytelling can engage the 5 senses and stir the imagination. Whether it's your personal story, a story you've heard, or a story from the Bible, stories are a great way to relate to your audiences and pack emotion into your presentation.

> *Audiences appreciate information but they lean in and listen to stories.*

Learn to tell an aspect of your story that can bring home a certain point. Don't be afraid to be vulnerable. People identify with honesty. This will win your audience over to your side, letting them know, if you can make it, they can, too. You are the author of your God-story. Nobody can tell your story like you can.

You are the only person on the planet with your story. Your voice is unique and special. You deserve to be heard. Don't shrink back but step into the spotlight and celebrate your God story today. As you share, you'll see the results of how your story can encourage others.

Be a giver. The best communicators I know share information openly and with a great deal of generosity. Not only do they demonstrate a wealth of information, the best communicators absolutely love the process of pouring into the lives of others. Do all you can to bring out the best in others, revealing your heart along with the information you want to deposit in your audience. Remember these two words: information and affirmation. So, when you stand before an audience, share not only what you know, but reveal why knowing it is important to you and why it's changed your life. Remember, the pulpit or platform is not a place to beat people down with your words. Refrain from sharing your 'dirty laundry' or airing your grievances. Always use the platform as a means to build people up and add value to their lives.

Do all you can to bring out the best in others, revealing your heart along with the information you want to deposit in your audience. Remember these two words: information and affirmation.

Be prepared. I've addressed this before, but it bears repeating. The more you practice, the more comfortable you'll be when standing in front of a room full of people. Look for ways to get in more practice. I spend a lot of time in my car so I rehearse my story-telling while I'm in traffic. You may also consider joining a speakers group. Volunteer to speak in front of audiences who know you, such as your family or your Sunday school class. They will be certain to cheer you on. Use these 'safe' audiences to help develop your message. Often we don't know if our performance really connects with our audience until we try it on for size in front of people who can give us honest feedback. It's a good thing to do a trial run in front of an audience of friends. Someone said if you're nervous, to look over people's heads as if you were looking at a clock on the back wall. I like the opposite approach.

I like to approach my performances as if everyone in the room is my best friend. I look people right in their eyes as if I were looking into their souls, speaking or singing with compassion, right to their pain. Everybody, without a doubt, is going through something. With the help of the Holy Spirit, you can speak right to the heart of the matter. Your message will resonate and your words will make a deep impact.

CALL TO ACTION

It's such a privilege to lift up people with encouraging words. Do all you can today to build people up whether you are on stage speaking to a roomful of strangers or in the company of close friends. When you are in the business of blessing people, your efforts never come back empty. I want to pray for you now that you will know more and more, the power of encouraging words.

Heavenly Father,

Everywhere we look we see people in pain. At work, at church at the gas station – no matter where we are, we meet people who are battling something as if their very lives depended on it. We know how they feel because we have to fight our own battles.

But we don't despair! We are convinced that You are our hope and salvation! Help those of us who believe in You to minister out of our own experience with You. You have never failed us and You never will. We have no reason to go through life with our heads hung low. But we rejoice, knowing that our situations are not over our heads but under my feet! Thank You, Father!

In Jesus' name,

Amen

CHAPTER 5

BE A LEADER

Do nothing out of selfish ambition or vain conceit.
Rather, in humility, value others above yourselves.
Philippians 2:3

eadership looks different depending on the situation, but at its most basic element, a leader is one who has the ability to establish a following of a team of individuals. If you turn around and there's somebody in your shadow the possibility is great they are following you.

You might say, "Babbie, I'm shy and reserved. I'm pretty sure I'm not a leader." Think again. In the most basic sense, leadership is about bringing out the best in the team. Leaders are intent on making life better for those in their sphere of influence. Great leaders are passionate about serving others and sharing tools for success. We can all do that. Right? While some believe that great leaders are born, I believe the potential to be a great leader lies within all of us. If you have the desire and the capability to influence others in a positive way, then you are a potential leader.

Leaders can be a CEO of a corporation, a pastor of a church, an elementary school teacher in charge of her classroom, a grocery store produce manager, or a mom in charge of the day to day duties of running a household. Certainly, if you are in ministry, if you have a message you desire to share with people in need, a vision or inspiration to impart to those around you, then it's vital that you develop your skills as a leader. To maximize your God-given potential as a leader, use your gifts and talents to bring out the best in others.

One of my favorite servant leaders is Bishop Jim Lowe. He is the author of a great book on maximizing your life called, Achieving Your Divine Potential. He is a pastor, songwriter and a leader in his church and community. In his book, he says, "God wouldn't give you a commission to live your life

"God wouldn't give you a commission to live your life in His image and likeness if He didn't give you the potential to accomplish it."

Bishop Jim Lowe

in His image and likeness if He didn't give you the potential to accomplish it." He goes on to give us a few more directives. "Act now – time is precious. So, stop making excuses. Refuse to listen to the world's attempt to limit your abilities. Hear and obey the Word of God. See yourself as a reflection of God on the earth and live like it. "

That's the kind of leader I want to be - a leader who can 'see it' in my mind before it becomes a reality. That was the kind of leader David was. He was a man of vision with keen insights and abilities to bring out the best in others.

While King Saul had the potential, he was someone who never fulfilled his destiny because he was blinded by his own personal struggle. He couldn't take his eyes off of himself long enough to see the value of those around him. Easily threatened by the gifts of others and often intimidated by their successes, King Saul led others through his weaknesses.

Up to this very day, those weaknesses have defined and tainted his legacy. David, however, was a pioneer, possessing the ability to blaze a trail for others to follow. He was a self-starter, initiating plans and processes as well as a goal-setter who could finish what he started.

As King Saul's armor-bearer, David certainly must have had the foresight to anticipate the needs of the king and the ability to see each need through to the finish. David did have his weaknesses, but his strengths seemed to outshine them. He was at his best when he was bringing out the best in others. His gifts flourished when he was leading others to a place of victory and accomplishment. This great man readily confessed the reason for his success in Psalm 18:31-32. "For who is God besides the Lord? And who is the Rock except our God? It is God who arms me with strength and keeps my way secure."

David must have been a very patient man. He was anointed king of Israel when he was a teenager and a shepherd. But David would have to wait many years before God's promise to him would actually come to pass.

This should be of great encouragement to you. Don't be in a hurry to get where God wants to take you. The Lord is always at work and much of that work will take real time to develop. It is natural to hasten toward the end result. But you can't have the product without the process. God is orchestrating something great behind the scenes. So remain patiently obedient whether you see results or not. Greatness is achieved over time and with thoughtful diligence.

Take the limits and the boundaries off of your dreams because God's plan for you is bigger than you can imagine. Keep in mind, while you have a dream, God has a plan. While you are waiting on the Lord, remember what you are waiting for. The old saints in my father's church use to say, "Serving the Lord will pay off after awhile". There is so much truth to that! God's plan may not look precisely like what you've envisioned and it may not take place within your time frame. But this is for certain. Everything God has planned for you is worth the wait because everything God planned for you is good. Remember Isaiah 55:8. "For my thoughts are not your thoughts, neither are your ways my ways," declares the Lord." NIV. Don't put yourself or God in a nice box, convincing yourself that God's plan can only be carried out in conventional ways.

Take the limits and the boundaries off of your dreams because God's plan for you is bigger than you can imagine.

Nor should you allow others to define the process. You might not see your dream modeled on the church stage. That's okay. The church can have a limited view and that limited view has a tendency to acknowledge certain kinds of gifts. Don't let that, by any means, discourage you. There is a path for you. Just do what God has called you to do. You see, not only do His plans involve you, but all those in your sphere of influence will be impacted by your plans and decisions. You are blazing a trail for others to follow and blazing that trail will take time and patience. One day, when the plan comes together with precision, you'll be so glad you waited on God.

One of the greatest leaders I've ever known was my father, Rev. W. George Wade. Born in the cotton fields of Alabama in the 1920's and raised in the Delta of Mississippi, my father knew what it was like to work hard and stand strong even in the face of racism, financial hardship and a system that was unjust and unfair to Black people.

Just like my siblings and me, Dad was the child of a preacher. I think Dad, in his younger years, was running from God's call on his life but sometimes we have to go far from home so God can have us all to Himself. Dad was drafted into the United States Army and fought in Germany and Belgium during World-World ll. While fighting in enemy territory, Dad was taken as a prisoner of war. In captivity, he cried out to God. He bargained with God, saying, "God, if You deliver me from the hands of my enemies, I'll preach the gospel." Dad was able to escape from the enemy's camp and he kept his word. While my father was in the Army he fully committed his life to Christ and dedicated his life to the ministry of preaching the gospel.

After Dad came home from the war, in the mid 1940's our parents moved to Michigan. Soon after that Dad was called to pastor the Lily Missionary Baptist Church in Jackson, where he pastored for almost 40 years. I watched my parents raise my four siblings and me while leading a church of hard-working families with love and tremendous dedication.

Week in and week out, Sunday in and Sunday out, year in and year out, my parents led the people of the church, teaching them to love God and make a difference in the community and the world. My father was a great family man, a community leader, a county commissioner, a prison chaplain, and a college professor.

My mother worked tirelessly at home, in the community, working with other pastor's wives and as the first lady of the church, teaching the women and the young people in the music department. My parents were truly faithful and dedicated to the work of the church. To lead a community of church folk for 39 years in the same church takes grace and grit.

"If God be your partner, make your plans larger." Rev. W.G. Wade

I saw first hand many of the challenges my parents endured but they were able to faithfully navigate the numerous obstacles that pastors and first ladies face. Dad always closed his Sunday morning radio program with these words. "If God be your partner, make your plans larger." Leadership is not only taught but caught. I'm passing that on to you now.

Why do I tell you all of this? I want you to know that the work you are doing is worth it. Some days you'll be disappointed, hurt, misunderstood and tempted to join so many others who have quit. That's when you must realize that it will cost you more to quit than it will to keep going. Be reminded that God sees and He knows how hard you've worked and all you've invested to get where you are.

Some people don't recognize that, but God does. While some saw a young Black boy, destined to be a victim of racism, economic disadvantages and other adverse circumstances, God saw the man my father would become - a great warrior, a strong family man, a passionate pastor and an influential leader.

Way back when my dad was a young man working on a sharecropper's cotton farm, a young family man who was spat upon, cursed at, ridiculed and called everything but a child of God, the Lord saw a gifted man who rallied Black people to vote during the civil rights movement of the 1960's. God used my father to empower those under his leadership during the culture wars of the 1970's. A consistent voice of encouragement on radio and television during that time, he challenged the church to hold to God's unchanging hand. Throughout the economic downturn of the 1980's, Rev. W. G Wade was a consistent beacon of light to a community seeking direction. It took great courage to put his life on the line for his country on foreign soil, when he couldn't use the public restroom in his own hometown because of the color of his skin. But, God sees way down the road into the future. And because of my parents I am here today, carrying the torch in my leg of this race.

> " *Leadership is not just a thing I do at work. It's not a place I walk into and out of. Once we're leading according to the Spirit, we lead always.* "
> Dr. Steve Greene

As I look back on my parents' leadership style, I now understand that one of their greatest qualities was the ability to lead from the front lines with love. For more than twenty years, I've been privileged to host a television talk show called, Babbie's House. I get to interview some interesting people who are leaders in the church and in society today. One of those great leaders is Dr. Steve Greene, Executive Vice President of Charisma Media and the author of a wonderful book called, Love Leads. His words really resonate with me. "Leadership is not just a thing I do at work. It's not a place I walk into and out of. Once we're leading according to the Spirit, we lead always. We lead in all things and in all ways. If we do that according to the principles of love, then we're getting close to the heart of God."

There's a great deal to be learned from people like my parents and Dr. Steve Greene. Gifted leaders know they don't have all the ideas. But they create an environment where everyone can contribute their ideas and feel they are validated. Gifted leaders teach us always to have an open mind.

Only narrow-minded people prejudge others because of their nationality or criticize others because of the way they were brought up or how they worship. Those I consider great leaders are adept at adapting to change when the situation calls for it. I'll admit, I still have so much to learn, because that mindset was challenged one night when I was in the local Piggly Wiggly grocery store.

Late one Sunday evening I made a quick run to the local grocery store to buy milk and bread for the upcoming week. As I was purchasing my items in the checkout line, I noticed a young, White man who had stepped into the line behind me. Dressed in greasy overalls, a dingy t-shirt rolled up at the sleeves, a ball cap placed low on his brow and a wad of tobacco chew rolled in his jaw, I felt a growing discomfort. Fear will always make you think the worst of people. Won't it? I quickly wrote a check for my few items and hastened to leave the store. I did not want to be in the parking lot with this man, alone, late at night. I was gathering up my bags when the man spoke to me.

He said, in his long southern drawl, "Excuse me ma'am. Are you....the gospel singer...Babbie Mason?" I hesitated, but acknowledged that I was. The man's face lit up like a Christmas tree as he exclaimed, "Praise God, sister! I LOVE your music!" Do you see? I was guilty of doing to this man precisely what had been done to me, my parents and other Black people. I had prejudged him based on his appearance when all along, this man was my brother in Christ. Do you see how easy it is to prejudge others because of your own experiences? I put a stop to it that night in the parking lot of the Piggly Wiggly when I prayed and asked God to change my heart.

Don't lag behind. If you lag behind you will be left behind.

My father's ministry is still making an impact although he graduated to heaven over 30 years ago. He passed away on March 4, 1987. Every year on that date, my siblings and I commemorate his passing by reminding one another to March Forth, to keep putting one foot in front of the other. To 'press toward the mark for the prize of the high calling of God in Christ Jesus'. Philippians 3:14 . I will include you in that greater family circle now. Don't lag behind. If you lag behind you will be left behind. You and I have technology, the internet, social media and smartphones to help us advance our noble causes and the kingdom of God. My parents had none of that. We don't have any excuses. Work hard and while you're working lead with love, faith and determination. March forth, my friend. March forth.

Here is more encouragement to help you become a better leader.

Have an open mind. First - don't go through life with a closed mind, a closed fist and preconceived notions. If you do, you'll miss out on a world of interesting people, traveling to exciting places and learning from new experiences. Mark Twain said,

"Travel is fatal to prejudice, bigotry and narrow-mindedness." It takes courage and bravery to break away from the pack, get out in the world and stretch your thinking. As a young girl, I thought all missionaries were White, single women who went off to places like Zambia and were never seen or heard of again! Talk about a preconceived notion! But God challenged my way of thinking and prodded me to open my eyes, my hands, my heart and my wallet. Do you know what I learned? I found that a missionary can even be a Black, married, mother and grandmother from the city. A missionary can be someone like you and me.

Remember, there are no conditions to the Great Commission.

Have global vision. Do this assignment today. Take a look in the mirror then ask this question. "Am I a missionary or a mission project?" Remember, there are no conditions to the Great Commission. Don't question. Just go! If you can't go overseas on a mission trip, get involved in an on-going project in your own home town. Go. Send. Give. Pray. Just do something!

God is looking for someone who will make a great commotion of the Great Commission.

I heard this great quote recently, "The mark of a great church is not in how many it seats but in how many it sends." Charles and I have taken many foreign mission trips over the years. Each time I returned home there was a bit of envy in my heart for those missionaries who have committed to a life of spreading the gospel on foreign soil, for they are where a lot of the action is. God is looking for someone who will make a great commotion of the Great Commission. **That person is you!**

Have a big heart. Understand that while you are leading, you are serving. A servant leader will always find joy in helping others to succeed. Whether that person works beside you as a peer, as a supervisor or a subordinate, give those you lead the love and respect they deserve. Everyone can thrive in that kind of environment.

CALL TO ACTION

Today is a day to lead with encouraging words. You will never know the power of encouraging others until you learn to encourage yourself. Do just like David did when he and his men returned home to Ziklag only to find their city burned to the ground and their families kidnapped by their enemies. His own men threatened to stone him. But the Bible says in 1 Samuel 30:6. "And David was greatly distressed; for the people spake of stoning him, because the soul of all the people was grieved, every man for his sons and for his daughters: but David encouraged himself in the LORD his God." Make it a point to encourage someone today, even if that someone is you. Join me in prayer for the gift of encouraging words.

Gracious God,

You are so patient with us. We tend to be so slow in learning the most important lessons in life. Help us to understand that others are following us as we follow Christ. Please tenderize our cold and stony hearts, Lord. In this selfish and cruel world help us to to lead with love and compassion. We know the power of love because we know You. Through a kind word, a smile, a simple act of kindness or a joyful affirmation, we will be looking for opportunities to compel others to come to You. That is our joy and privilege.

In Jesus' name,

Amen.

CHAPTER 6

BE A SERVANT

I have found David, son of Jesse, a man after my own heart; he will do everything I want him to do.
Acts 13:22

King David is most often painted in a favorable light. But he was a man of grievous faults. He was less than an ideal father. He had a weakness for beautiful women. And we can't broach the subject without mentioning his adulterous affair with Bathsheba and the plotted murder of her husband, Uriah.

In spite of all that, the Lord said of David in Acts 13:22, "I have found David, son of Jesse, a man after my own heart; he will do everything I want him to do." The foundation of David's relationship with God is found in the latter half of that verse; he will do everything I want him to do. God truly blessed David. The reason? David's heart was in the right place. A humble-hearted man, we only have to read David's many psalms to understand the tenderness of his heart toward God.

David had an abundance of talent. As we examine David's life and his relationship with God we can conclude, however, that God is not that impressed with talent. David had won over the hearts of kings and commoners alike. But, God isn't looking for people with popularity and a huge fan base. What God said of David, He desires of all of us, 'he will do everything I want him to do.' God is searching for a person, man or woman, who will do precisely what God asks, without question. He is searching for someone whose heart responds quickly and appropriately to personal sin. Then God is seeking to bless that one whose heart is sold out to Him regardless of the way the cultural tide is flowing. This attitude is called humility. A man of brute strength and confidence, David possessed humility – a meekness, a submissiveness and compliance to God.

What God said of David, He desires of all of us, 'he will do everything I want him to do.'

Every child of God must realize first and foremost that the way up is down. If you want to be great in the kingdom of God – learn to serve others. If your main motivation for being in any Christian ministry is for the big paycheck, the book or record sales, the royal treatment and the fame, the awards or the exposure, you may be happy for a while. But fame and popularity have a way of fading.

Decades after her death, Marilyn Monroe is still considered a Hollywood star and culture icon. Many authors and documentaries have revealed how she struggled to balance her real life against her manufactured Hollywood image. Her life has been described as a roller-coaster, checkered by drug abuse and a desire to be loved and validated. Her own words describe it best. "Fame doesn't fulfil you. It warms you a bit, but that warmth is temporary."

Fame is enticing, illusive and consuming. It's never enough. You'll go around and around in circles chasing futility only to land at emptiness. This is what happens when people worship other people. Those who worship become disenchanted and those who are worshipped are consumed. You see, people were never meant to be worshipped. Only God is worthy of worship. We are absolutely nothing apart from Him. To maximize your God-given potential as an ambassador of Christ, realize that Christian love is demonstrated by humbly serving God and people.

Jesus didn't often bring attention to His own personal attributes. However, in Matthew 11:28 we find Jesus drawing attention to His own humility. Matthew 11:28-29 Jesus said, "Come to Me, all who are weary and heavy-laden, and I will give you rest. Take My yoke upon you and learn from Me, for I am gentle and humble in heart, and you will find rest for your souls." NASB. Jesus could have boasted of His ability to raise the dead, feed the multitude or calm stormy seas while walking on water. However, of all the qualities Jesus could mention concerning Himself, He sheds a light on humility. If Jesus found it of utmost importance to live a life of humility here in the earth, then certainly this attitude and this attribute should be a prerequisite for the rest of us.

Have you ever noticed that arrogance always draws attention to itself? Arrogance always says, "Look at me as I make my fashionable entrance. Observe how I draw all the oxygen out of the room in an effort to get noticed! Here I am! It's all about me!" That's the mentality of many who seek success in the 21st century. Humility on the other hand, is always concerned about how to better others. A humble person defers to others and is not

Please don't confuse meekness with weakness. Jesus wasn't a wimp or a pushover and He's not asking you to be one. The opposite is true. Meekness is power under control.

concerned about promotion or looking to capitalize or manipulate a moment just for 15 seconds of fame. Now, you don't have to worry about promotion or recognition. Leave that to God. Read Psalm 75:6-7. "For promotion and power come from nowhere on earth, but only from God. He promotes one and deposes another." TLB Please don't confuse meekness with weakness. Jesus wasn't a wimp or a pushover and He's not asking you to be one. The opposite is true. Meekness is power under control. It does not mean to abandon one's own strength but meekness is rather yielding one's strength and will to God's control. Through the power of the Holy Spirit, we are all commanded to walk in submission to God.

We all need to examine our motives and determine why we want to be in ministry in the first place. It's easy to be drawn in by the hype and the allure of the bright lights. The applause of men, nice hotels, star treatment, awards and validation from adoring fans is very attractive. The fame and popularity are all really nice. I'm not going to deny that. But if it's fortune and fame you're after, be honest with yourself and the rest of us. Don't muddy the water by saying you're doing this for the sake of the Gospel because the heart of the Gospel is winning those who are lost to the saving knowledge of Christ.

Don't get me wrong. I'm not against signing with a label, being a part of the music industry, selling records or winning awards. I've done all of that. It's a blessing to be recognized by my peers and I am truly grateful for the opportunity and the exposure it has given this ministry. Being on a record label opened many doors for me – doors to minister to people all over the world.

At the end of the day, the main motivation for a call to ministry in the first place must be about helping people find God. Only He can meet their needs. All it took for me to understand the importance of that, was a letter like the one I received from an admirer. Let me tell you the story.

At the end of the day, the main motivation for a call to ministry in the first place must be about helping people find God. Only He can meet their needs.

I had been a guest of Moody Radio's Friday Night Sing, a concert that is broadcast LIVE over the Moody Radio Network. During the concert, I sang the powerful song called He'll Find A Way, written by my dear friend and longtime songwriting buddy, Donna Douglas Walchle.

The chorus says:

> If He can paint a sunset
>
> And put the stars in place
>
> If He can raise up mountains
>
> And calm the storm-tossed waves
>
> If He can conquer death forever
>
> To open heaven's gates

I know for you, I know for you

He'll find a way

The next week I received a letter in the mail from a young lady who told me that on that same Friday night, she was on her way to a nearby lake not far from her home. She had a gun in her car and had planned to take her life. As she drove toward the lake she turned on the radio and hit the scan button. The radio landed on a station that was broadcasting my concert on Moody Radio. The words and music she heard coming through the radio deeply touched her heart as she sat in her car with the loaded gun in her hand. After I had finished singing, she prayed and asked God to help her. She got out of the car and heaved the gun into the lake. The words to the song gave her hope to trust God with her circumstances and she wrote to tell me what the song had meant to her.

Now, I have won awards and trophies, but they don't compare to people, trophies of grace, whose lives have been touched and changed by the power of the gospel of Jesus Christ.

Over the years I have received countless letters, emails, phone calls and comments on social media, reminding me of the power in music that celebrates the hope we have in Jesus. I have received emails from those who have told me they listen to my music during chemo treatments.

I have several pictures that were taken at the graveside of loved ones, where the lyrics to the song, Trust His Heart, were chiseled on that loved one's headstone. I have sung at the bedside of a woman who was a hospice patient. Her dying request was to hear the lyrics of a song God had blessed me to compose or record. I received a letter from a mother, pregnant with twins, who was on bedrest during the last trimester of her pregnancy. She told me she listened to my music daily, to get her through those last few months. I spoke with a middle-aged woman whose mother has alzheimer's disease. Sometimes her mother would become disoriented and cry out in fits of rage. She told me that one of the things that would calm her mother's spirit was listening to my music. I met a young man who was saved at one of my concerts. He is in ministry today. Now, I have won awards and trophies, but they don't compare to people, trophies of grace, whose lives have been touched and changed by the power of the gospel of Jesus Christ.

Practically speaking, I'm often asked of music upstarts, "Babbie, how do I get the attention of a label so I can get a record deal? Should I do a demo and make it available online? Design a website? Get new photographs, a booking agent or a manager?" I don't frown upon any of that. Seeking the attention of music label executives is a great goal if that's the direction you want to head. That model still works in many cases. The Internet, however, has changed the way music is produced, promoted, sold and distributed. Launching your ministry endeavors online as an independent artist or self-published author and driving your message with social media can prove to be a valid way to touch a lot of people and even get the attention of labels or publishers. These companies are very selective of those they sign.

They consider the person's age, appearance and their popularity online. Record label executives will want to hear the quality of your original music because this could be an asset to their company's bottom line. Book publishers may consider things such as your writing and public speaking style, demographics, unit sales from other books and your availability to travel.

If you want to get the attention of publishers or record label executives, go where they are. Attend industry-level conferences where you can meet people, establish professional relationships and get a better understanding of expectations. As you increase your visibility, you'll increase your credibility and your knowledge.

The old model meant that recording or publishing companies put up the money for the project's budget, but in return, owned the artist's record masters, book manuscripts, soundtracks, music publishing copyrights, name, photos and likeness, while the artist or author still had to hit the road to sell products while earning only a few cents on each unit sold. While this is one option, you have more options now than ever before.

Should you choose to go the route of the independent artist, for example, using the internet to promote your music and message, you can have complete control over your career. If you have music you wish to promote, then you must act as the record company. If you have written a book you wish to promote, then you, in essence, are the publisher. You are responsible for every detail concerning the direction of your products.

The internet is not your source. It's only a resource.

This is where ministry turns into business really fast. The internet is a great tool and offers countless ways to reach a global audience with the click of a button on your computer or cell phone. With all the numerous platforms available to reach your audience with your music and your message, doing everything on your own can be a daunting task. Start small by making a plan.

Consider using social media as a way to connect with your

audience. After that, consider building your own website. Consider recording single songs instead of a 10-song album or CD. You'll save a great deal of money, while still using your music to impact people. If you don't have concert dates on the calendar, use online platforms to post your music and make it available for others to enjoy. Little by little, step by step, you will make headway. You will introduce your music to a global platform and be a blessing to others. As you are considering how you'll build your online presence, remember this. The internet is not your source. It's only a resource.

Maybe you're not a good fit for a label or a major publishing company. It could be that your music or book got rejected by them. That's okay. Take control of your destiny by working hard to improve your skill as a singer, songwriter or author. Develop your own business, producing your own music or self-publishing your own book.

I like to look at the creative process with the mentality that a music recording or book project is forever. Approach the project with the mindset that you'll 'do it right the first time.' This way, you won't waste valuable time and money by going back to fix what you've already recorded or written. So a commitment to excellence on every level is a must. Only you and the Lord know what motivates you. Examine your heart and determine why you want to establish a public ministry in the first place. Remember, only what you do for Christ will last. And only what you do for people will make a difference.

As far as projects are concerned, I only want to create books, Bible studies and music I believe will have a long-lasting impact on people. The products I created from the mid-70's right up to this moment, live on today because, with the help of God, they were written, performed and produced with excellence.

Ultimately, it's Christ we want to please. Many of the songs I've written have been translated in over 20 languages and recorded by other artists. I started writing books and Bible studies in recent years. Now they are being published in other languages as well. As far as the writers, producers, musicians, editors and anyone else on my creative team is concerned, our job is to create excellent work to the best of our ability, promote it as best as we can so we can impact more people, then leave the rest to God.

A young lady came to me after I had sung at a Sunday morning worship service aboard the Logos Hope, a ship operated on behalf of Operation Mobilization, a non-profit mission organization. The young lady was from South Korea. She held a song book in her hand while she told me that my song, With All My Heart, was sung by thousands in her church back home in Seoul. Then she turned to the page where the song, With All My Heart, was printed. Because the words were written in Korean, the only things I could comprehend were the letters in my own name and the music notation on the page. Here's my point. Commit everything you do with excellence. You never know where your work will end up or how it will serve others at home and abroad.

Not only should the content be written and recorded with excellence but the presentation must represent excellence as well. Concerning photographs, nothing less than the best will do. Photographs, like recordings, live on forever. So put your best face out there. Oftentimes, the photo is the first point of contact you'll make with your audience. A dear friend told me that before we met, she saw my recording on a bookstore shelf. She had never

Concerning photographs, nothing less than the best will do.

heard of me before but bought my recording merely because the cover photo, the project's artwork and design were appealing. The artwork and design were so well done that the cover seemed to draw her.

Your photo may represent you on the covers of your music projects, on your website and social media sites, business cards, postcards, books, magazine interviews, church bulletins and marquis, billboards, television and all over the internet. Your friend may have a cell phone that takes nice pictures. But, I implore you to hire professionals whenever you can, to help create a polished public image. I'm sure you can tell at a glance, the difference between a project that has that professional touch and one that appears to be home-made by an amateur.

Remember that old adage? "You get what you pay for." It's true. Just as it's important to use a qualified producer and the finest players to record your music, always hire a good photographer who can capture your best impression. Using the right lighting, the correct lens and great composition, a professional photographer will help to communicate the 'story' you want to portray to your audience.

Some people may dismiss this, but I never, ever do a photoshoot without professionals to help me with hair, make-up and wardrobe. I also recommend that you hire a professional graphic designer and printer for your printing needs so everything you put online, present on stage, or put into people's hands is consistent with your overall brand.

Don't have money for professional photographs, a

Payment doesn't have to always come in the form of cash money. If you own a business, a product or provide a service, consider bartering.

new website, business cards, postcards or recordings? We know Rome wasn't built in a day. You'll need to prioritize. Decide what you need now and what can wait until later. Payment doesn't have to always come in the form of cash money. If you own a business, a product or provide a service, consider bartering. It may take a little more work to find those who might take you up on a bartering agreement. But, I assure you, the possibilities are out there.

All the things I just mentioned are very helpful when it comes to promoting your ministry or business. But, honestly speaking, you don't need any of that to minister to people.

The only thing that's really required to touch the hearts of people is a desire to use whatever talent you have to tell others about Jesus. That's all! You may not get a paycheck, but that's okay. You'll get paid in a thousand ways money could never buy. The moment may not produce a photo opportunity you can share online, but all of heaven will throw a party when someone gives their life to Christ as a result of your service. I promise you, when you serve, you'll actually find immense joy in helping others who may not ever be able to help you in return. God notices, however. I know this first hand. He has afforded me countless opportunities to sing for people in all kinds of situations. On many, many occasions I didn't get a check for my services. But I

> *The only thing that's really required to touch the hearts of people is a desire to use whatever talent you have to tell others about Jesus. That's all!*

came away blessed. Let me share another story with you.

I went to visit a dear relative who is a resident at a senior retirement home. She and I visited for a while in her small but quite adequate apartment. After a short visit, I wheeled her up to the spacious gathering room and prepared to leave. On the other side of the room, I noticed a grand piano. There's something about a piano just sitting against the wall in a corner that always draws me to play it. So I walked over to the administration desk and asked the lady at the counter if I could play the piano. She seemed delighted at the suggestion.

She told me that a local pastor would arrive in a few moments to lead an afternoon worship service for the residents but I was welcome to play and sing until the pastor arrived. I walked over to the piano, sat down and began to play and sing some familiar hymns. One by one, beginning with my family member, residents wheeled themselves over near the piano and began to sing along with me. Others were pushed in their wheelchairs by a nurse.

In a matter of moments, the gathering room was full of people; residents, nurses and visitors, all singing hymns and clapping their hands. Many months later, I saw one of the ladies who works at the facility. She told me those few moments of singing around the piano were some of the most memorable moments she has ever experienced on her job.

On another occasion, I was invited to attend the monthly meeting of a local songwriter's group in a nearby city. The group held their monthly meetings in a local bar. When I arrived at the location, I was a bit hesitant to go inside, but I had given the association president my word. So I went inside the bar and found a table. My host was on stage playing some bluegrass music with his band.

A few songs into their set, he said, "There's a nice lady

joining us tonight. I'm gonna ask her to come up and sing a song for us. Babbie Mason come on up and sing with us!" With no rehearsal, I asked the band to back me up. I sang a few verses of Amazing Grace. When I was finished, someone from the back of the room shouted, "Sing another one!" So the band and I sang a few verses of "Just a Closer Walk With Thee." Again, somebody shouted, "Sing How Great Thou Art." There was another request for "Shout To The Lord". For 30 more minutes, the band and I took requests and sang worship songs in the bar. Afterwards, I took my seat. People came by the table to express their gratitude. We prayed with several people and even led two people to the Lord. A few days later, I received a barrage of emails asking me when I'd be making another appearance at the bar to jam with the band!

Whether you plan to use your talents on a volunteer basis or you hope to eventually get paid for your services, make ministry your main motivation. Real ministry is never about you. Ministry always acquiesces to the needs of others. If you want to be great in the kingdom of God, learn to be the servant of all. Some tend to think of servanthood as drudgery or dirty work. But, truly, you will never be more like Jesus than when you are serving others. You will find no greater joy in ministry than being a blessing to someone else. When we bring out the best in others, somehow we bring out the best in ourselves. May I suggest some other volunteer opportunities you could explore?

Volunteer to sing or lead a Bible study at a local jail or prison.

Make yourself available to lead worship for a neighborhood Bible Study. Better yet, host a small group Bible study in your own home where you can lead worship and share with others. Sing on your church worship team or play in the church band or orchestra – for free. Lead worship for your church or Sunday school class or for Vacation Bible School.

Play or sing for patients at a local hospital or for patrons at a local restaurant. Volunteer to lead worship at a church that has no music minister or worship team.

Offer to play or sing for free during worship services for those in the Armed Services. Make yourself available to sing for a teenage crisis pregnancy center, retirement village, drug rehab or local homeless shelter.

I have to tell you one last story. Years ago, in the early days of our ministry, Charles and I were invited to Ft. Lauderdale, Florida, where I would be singing for a convention. Upon our arrival, we were blown away by the hospitality of our hosts. They sent a chauffeur-driven limousine to pick us up at the airport and take us to the hotel where we'd be staying during our visit. On the ride to the hotel, we admired the beautiful homes on the waterfront and the expensive yachts cruising in the harbor.

I nudged Charles and whispered, "Man, I could sure get used to this kind of treatment!" Once we turned onto the hotel property, my eyes filled with wonder as we cruised down the long, tree-lined drive to the hotel entrance. Lush tropical flowers and shrubs decorated the green turf. When I glanced out of the window of the limo again, I saw something that shocked me. I couldn't believe my eyes. Nestled in the meticulously designed landscape was a homeless man, fast asleep on the perfectly manicured grass. My heart was deeply pierced. The contrast of a homeless man sleeping just feet away from an air-conditioned room, a clean bed, a hot shower and room service, was more than my heart could bear.

I sensed the Lord saying to me, "You can enjoy all the good things I have in store for you. But the perks are not why I have called you. Remember, you are to feed the hungry, clothe the naked, bind up those who are bruised, befriend the lonely and spread the gospel. Remember the reasons why you are called." Once, the car came to a stop, I walked over to the spot where I had seen the man, but he was gone. I learned some important lessons that day.

The way up is down. If you want to be great in God's kingdom, serve others. God is looking for people with a heart like His. He is searching for people who seek to serve rather than be served. Commit 2 Chronicles 16:9 to memory. "For the eyes of the Lord roam to and fro throughout the earth seeking a heart that is faithful to him that He might fully support it." Endeavor to be that person.

The way out is in. To continually enjoy peace in your life, make time to be in God's presence, praying to Him and listening to Him. Be mindful to keep sin and its distraction at bay. When you do miss the mark and commit a sinful act, keep short accounts with the Lord, immediately asking His forgiveness the moment you have committed sin against Him. David demonstrated how he treasured the Word of God in Psalm 119:11. "Thy word have I hid in mine heart, that I might not sin against thee."

The way through is over. Our adversary will do all he can to ensnare you with guilt and shame from your past. Jesus came to set you free of anything that enslaves you. So get over your mistakes and move on! Get over your past and thank God for the gift of the present. Get over your weaknesses and start focusing on your strengths. Don't let your issues stand in the way of allowing God to use you.

Read David's passionate prayer in Psalm 51:10-13. "Create in me a clean heart, O God; and renew a right spirit within me. Cast me not away from thy presence; and take not thy holy spirit from me. Restore unto me the joy of thy salvation; and uphold me with thy free spirit. Then will I teach transgressors thy ways; and sinners shall be converted unto thee." The same kind of servant potential lies within you. You are no different. God saw the servant in David and God sees the servant within you.

CALL TO ACTION

Today, commit to embracing the mindset of a servant. No, it's not popular today to assume the position of a servant, preferring others ahead of ourselves. But there really is so much joy to be found when you are a blessing to others. So, move from thinking about it to doing something about it. Don't wait to be asked, but find a ministry or other organization where you can invest your time, your talent and your treasure.

You don't need a college degree, money, a recorded music project or multiple reasons. You only need the desire to make the world better one person at a time. Find yourself while losing yourself in the service of others.

Shortly after our trip to Ft. Lauderdale where I saw the homeless man asleep in the hotel landscape, I composed these words in the song, Show Me How To Love, written back in 1988. Make these words your prayer today.

Be A Servant

Heavenly Father,

Show me how to love in the true meaning of the word

Teach me to sacrifice, expecting nothing in return

I want to give my life away

Becoming more like You each and every day

My words are not enough

Show me how to love

In Jesus' name,

Amen

CHAPTER 7

BE CREATIVE

"Behold, I have seen a son of Jesse the Bethlehemite who is a skillful musician, a mighty man of valor, a warrior, one prudent in speech, and a handsome man; I Samuel 16:18

Imagine if you can, walking a mile in David's sandals. While David held King Saul in high esteem, Saul grew to deeply despise David. His affinity for David soon turned to intense jealousy with David's growing popularity among the Hebrew nation. David's reputation as a warrior was impressive. Not only had he slayed Goliath, David had also annihilated 10,000 of the enemy's fighters.

Once Saul became suspicious that David would ascend to the throne as king, Saul would do anything within his power to prevent this from happening. But David's dynamic magnetism could not be stopped. Saul's daughter Michal became one of David's wives and Jonathan, Saul's son, became David's best friend. Jealousy and envy will make a man do the unthinkable. Severely threatened and no longer able to handle David's approval rating, Saul's anger reached a boiling point. King Saul attempted to extinguish David on numerous occasions. Once in a violent rage Saul tried to take David out with a spear. David finally got the message and would have to devise a plan, flee the palace and become a man on the run. David would spend years as a fugitive, running all over Israel, hiding in caves and trenches, with Saul in hot pursuit.

Have you ever had to reboot or change your plans in midstream when your original plan didn't work out? We have all been there. Flexible thinking demands that you look at your situation from every perspective. It could even be crucial to your growth and success. Every time a major change happens in life such as losing a job, a loved one passes, you face retirement, the bottom drops out of the economy, a health challenge occurs or some other major shift happens, you must adjust to the change or risk encountering a setback.

Create a plan, but within that plan, leave room for inspiration and imagination.

A rigid mindset will certainly bring progress to a screeching halt. Life changes. People change. Circumstances change. Make the decision right now to implement creative thinking as you initiate future plans and projects because this mindset will keep your dream afloat. Create a plan, but within that plan, leave room for inspiration and imagination. **To maximize your God-given potential as a creative person, be open-minded and think out of the box.**

Creativity has consistently been a driving force in my life and ministry. I've always believed any success I've enjoyed was greatly due to my ability to be creative with the gifts God gave me.

I've always found it natural to meet head on, the opportunities that were presented to me, and if I had to reinvent myself, then that was a part of completing that assignment.

I have never wanted to miss out on any opportunities that were presented to me. There has always been this pervasive thought resting in the back of my mind, that I will somehow be held accountable for the work I did or didn't do here on earth. A deep desire to please God has always been a huge motivation. And this pertains to all of us. If we desire to please Him, God will give us more opportunity.

Remarkably, I have found, everything I needed was already within reach. The creativity, the motivation, the passion to get it done, the ideas, the ability – everything was already on the inside of me. God already put them there. The same is true of you. This is why you must never lose hope or throw in the towel. When life knocks you down, there will always be a reason to get up, brush yourself off and try again. Remember, the resources you need are already within you, waiting for you to call on them. You only need to take inventory of those resources, tap into the power within you and put those resources to work.

Not long ago, at the end of a long day, Charles and I were tired from the day's work. I really didn't feel much like cooking. Besides, I looked in the cupboards and didn't see much to cook. I suggested we go out for dinner.

Charles, on the other hand, expressed his displeasure at the thought of going out to eat. He said he would go in the kitchen and find something to prepare for dinner. I am never concerned when Charles Mason goes into the kitchen to cook. I don't know how my dear husband does it. But he has the ability to make something masterful, seemingly out of nothing. He went into the cupboard and got a little of this. He went to the refrigerator and got some of that. Then he went to the freezer and grabbed a bag of the other. The next thing I knew I was sitting down to the table before a meal that was truly fit for a queen.

That is the picture of your life. Every ingredient you'll ever need is waiting for you to access it. I think about Charles' process when preparing our meal. He had to do some creative thinking, some searching and some moving things around to find the necessary items to prepare our dinner. I know he had to resort to some hand-me down recipes from his past, combined with some ingenuity from the present. But that's how you get it done. Too often we rely on a quick fix, an easy gimmick or someone else's plan when what we need to do is take inventory of what we already have in order to create a masterpiece.

Think about what you have at your fingertips right now. Your life is comprised of your own story along with memories and experiences from your past. Good or bad, you have a wealth of experiences God can use to bring you joy and help others. He wants to use your story for His glory. What about your relationships? I know you have parents who have influenced you. Do you have grandparents and extended family whose lives have impacted you in some way? Certainly there are teachers, employers, ministers and a plethora of others who have taught you some invaluable life lessons. You can write about what they have taught you. You can sing about all you have learned and experienced. God has endowed you with a depth of emotions. Pull on your greatest times of joy from your childhood. Dig into your memories and your funniest experiences. Even those times of tremendous pain, loss and immense sadness will help you express your story in your book, blogs, on stage or online.

Don't even think for a moment that your story doesn't matter. There will always be someone out there who needs to hear what you have to say. What do you have in your hand that God can use? Moses had a staff. With it, he parted waters. David has a sling and a stone. With it, he slayed a giant. A young boy had 2 fish and 5 loaves in a lunch bag. With it, thousands were fed. A widow had an empty barrel and a handful of meal. Her obedience sustained her through a lengthy drought. Just ask yourself, "What do I have in my hand right now?" When you release what is in your hand, God will

Don't even think for a moment that your story doesn't matter. There will always be someone out there who needs to hear what you have to say.

release what is in His hand. Not in a drip. Not in a drizzle. Not in a drop. But in a deluge! It's His way to overwhelm you with His holy ability on the inside of you. You and God - that is when the miraculous happens.

When I first got started in music ministry, I wasn't on a record label at the time so I decided to record on my own. Over a period of time I saved up some money and people who loved our ministry even made some contributions. Before long I had enough money to go into the studio to record. Making a recording is a big task!

Before the first session was arranged, I met with my producer and the studio engineer who helped me to book the best musicians my money could buy. After all the recording was finished, I had to approve all the mixes and arrange for the photo shoot. The name of the project had to be decided.

I had to determine the order of all the songs, write album liner notes, approve the artwork and arrange for manufacturing and shipping of products. I remember the day back in 1977, when the shipment of my first record arrived. A big semi-truck pulled up in front of my apartment and the driver unloaded what seemed to be an endless number of boxes. It was a bit scary, wondering if I would be able to sell those albums. I worked hard, though. I sold albums to bookstores on a consignment basis. I sold albums after my concerts. I even sold albums out of the trunk of my car. Soon, I was placing an order for another shipment. I made appointments with local radio stations and asked them to play my music. Some of the songs I recorded were written by other writers and some were my own compositions. That meant I had to step into the role of music publisher.

By the time I signed on with Word Records in 1989, I had produced five projects on my own. I was blessed to record for Word Records for ten years. I went on to establish a great working relationship with Spring Hill Music Group for five years. Interestingly, I started out as an independent music artist. Now, I've come full circle, joining the ranks of the independents once again. I tell you all this to let you know that wherever life takes you, you can embrace it. Whatever season you're in, God will provide for you there.

People ask me all the time about the process of writing a book or a song. My answer is simple. If you want to write, communicate about what you love. I write because I love singing and writing about all the Lord has done for me. I write because I enjoy encouraging others. Long before I was writing books and songs I wrote in my journals. I wrote stories and songs for my own children, newsletters for ministry supporters and songs for my classroom students. I wrote songs for the choirs I worked with. So how do you become a writer? You just write! You have to develop the discipline. That means you must write every day.

Make it a habit and a practice. Start by writing a blog or create Facebook posts on a regular basis. Your posts could even serve as chapters in a book down the line. And when you think your work is good enough, showcase it before an audience.

When you attend our LIVE event for singers, songwriters and authors, called the Inner Circle, you'll learn more about how to jump-start your music ministry, improve your songwriting, record and promote your music, publish your books and get your work into the marketplace.

Bottom line, if you don't have all the information you need to advance your work, go where you can find it. Do an internet search. Attend a conference. Listen to a webinar. Read a book. Enter a competition. Do whatever it takes to get the feedback and the information you need. I understand if you are hesitant to showcase your work for fear of rejection. But, with time and determination, you'll gain confidence to showcase your music.

Life will often pull the rug out from under you, causing you to think on your feet or catch yourself on the way down. Pursuing God's plan is not about being comfortable, but about being compliant to the will and the purpose of God. Do you think David was at ease in King Saul's palace? Not when the king was manic-depressive, irrational and emotionally unstable. But David was certainly called to serve him. Tight and uncomfortable situations force you to think on your feet, to be resourceful and use your creative imagination. When you do that, you will find

Pursuing God's plan is not about being comfortable, but about being compliant to the will and the purpose of God.

where God leads He precedes. He is already ahead of you, making the way.

The Prophet Elijah was doing the will and the work of the Lord when he found himself in a real confrontation, standing against 450 false prophets of Baal. Read the amazing story beginning at 1 Kings 18:20. At Mount Carmel, we find a showdown between the Prophet Elijah, a man sent by God and a multitude of idol worshippers along with an assembly of false prophets backed by the evil queen, Jezebel. We are familiar with the story of how each side erected an altar to its deity and prayed to the heavens to rain down fire to prove which one was the true God. The false prophets prayed to their god, tore their clothes, even cut themselves until they drew blood, but their god never answered them. Elijah did what he was led to do to prove His God was Almighty and All-powerful.

Elijah ordered that the sacrifice be drenched with water and even had a trench dug around the sacrifice to contain it all. When he prayed to his God (and ours), a ferocious fire fell from heaven and consumed Elijah's sacrifice followed by a proclamation from all the people that declared, "The Lord, He is God!" Vs. 39 KJV.

He then ordered that all the false prophets be seized and executed. Backed by the power of God, Elijah stood toe to toe with a powerful force and lived to tell about it. No doubt, this epic event was a defining moment in Elijah's life and ministry.

Can you recall some defining moments of your own? Those moments may feel as if you are being stretched beyond what you think you can bear. But just like Elijah, when you need it most, you will discover the power of God working in you. You will also discover some amazing strengths you didn't know you possessed. Keep a record of those stories - not just in your memory. Write them down. They will chronicle your life story and remind you of how God made a way for you. I'll never forget a defining moment in my life when I knew it was God who orchestrated a powerful turn of events.

Right after I had written the song, All Rise, I was still singing in the alto section of the choir in my home church. We had been invited to sing at an evangelism conference where we would sing All Rise in one of the evening services. The host church's sanctuary was packed, wall to wall, standing room only. During the service, our choir and I stood to sing the song. When we were finished, an otherwise conservative audience rose to their feet in worship.

There were hands lifted and audible shouts of praise. We sang All Rise four times that evening, even closing the service with the song. The whole event was captured on video tape and organically circulated across the convention, opening more doors of opportunity to sing the song in concerts and churches around the world. That was definitely a defining moment in my life.

At the Inner Circle, Charles and I share from our knowledge and experiences and we invite other music ministry and business professionals to join us in equipping independent singers, songwriters and self-published authors for ministry according to Ephesians 4:12.

By the late 80's people began seeking our counsel to help them get their ministries off the ground. We saw a great need in this area and decided to host our own music conference where we could dedicate an entire weekend to teaching, training and mentoring other musicians and writers.

We saw the value in helping upstarts learn to write better songs, avoid costly mistakes when launching their music ministries, find tools to help them understand the music business, better manage their careers, understand their calling, and take care of their voices for the long haul. The Babbie Mason Music Conference was born. The name has since been changed to The Inner Circle, but the concept remains intact. At the Inner Circle, Charles and I share from our knowledge and experiences and we invite other music ministry and business professionals to join us in equipping independent singers, songwriters and self-published authors for ministry according to Ephesians 4:12. Attendees from all over the world come to learn about the music ministry and industry, network with their peers, discover tools for self-publishing their books, get honest feedback on their original songs and performance techniques, and receive encouragement through worship and inspiring speakers. The internet is a tool that connects us all globally, and for the independent music artist and the self-published author, what was once only a possibility, can now become a reality.

I dreamed of how I could touch as many people as possible with more efficiency.

As the desire to train the next generation of singers, songwriters and authors became more of a passion, I began to pray about how I could impact this demographic more effectively. For several years, I prayed about what the next season of life and ministry might hold for me. I've always been one who wanted to help others be and do better. I dreamed of how I could touch as many people as possible with more efficiency. God gave me one of the biggest assignments I've ever embraced and that was to create Babbie Mason Radio (www. babbiemasonradio.com).

Today Babbie Mason Radio is an internet radio station, online 24 hours a day promoting the gospel with beautiful music and encouraging words. You'll hear my music, the stories behind my songs, messages from my books, Bible studies and devotionals. You'll also hear music and interviews from your favorite gospel music artists, great Christian programs featuring

In keeping with our vision, Babbie Mason Radio also embraces the music and the life-stories of independent music artists and self-published authors from around the world.

popular pastors, authors and ministry personalities, as well as music from our favorite old-school artists. In keeping with our vision, Babbie Mason Radio also embraces the music and the life-stories of independent music artists and self-published authors from around the world. Music artists and authors who are not on a major label or publishing roster now have a place where their music and message can be celebrated and validated on a global platform. Everybody is somebody on Babbie Mason Radio.

I knew the Lord was up to something big when I received a phone call from a good friend who checks in with me periodically. At the time, she asked me what projects I was working on so she could pray specifically for me. I told her I was building an internet radio station. She could hear the excitement in my voice concerning this new endeavor. She told me about an upcoming conference for women in radio and TV that she would be attending and asked if I wanted to attend with her. I checked my calendar and found I had the day free, so I decided to attend.

Besides, it would be fun to attend a conference where I wasn't on the program. That day proved to be the day that the dream and vision for Babbie Mason Radio became explicitly clear. My friend works for an international radio ministry and she shared our vision with some of her departmental leaders in that ministry.

Today, Babbie Mason Radio partners with that international radio ministry as well as other global ministries, taking the message of the gospel of Jesus Christ to the uttermost parts of the earth. Cities all over the United States and countries all over the world are exposed to great Christian music and powerful programs all centered on the message of the hope we have in Christ. I'm continually overwhelmed when I see the hits to the station's website from U.S cities like Spokane, New York City, Little Rock, Detroit, Charlotte, Atlanta, Syracuse, and Miami to faraway places like Russia, Ghana, Japan, South Africa, Australia, Great Britain, Brazil, the Caribbean Islands and other faraway places, too many to name here.

The internet is the new frontier. The need to share the gospel of Jesus Christ on this new frontier has never been more urgent and it's never been more exciting.

Did you know there are almost as many cell phone subscriptions (over 6.8 billion) as there are people on the planet (over 7 billion)? Forty percent of the world's population has an internet connection. In 1995, that statistic was less than 1%. More internet traffic is being carried on mobile devices today than ever before. Most homes in the United States have abandoned the land line and are totally dependent on the cell phone. The internet is the new frontier. The need to share the gospel of Jesus Christ on this new frontier has never been more urgent and it's never been more exciting. That's why it's so important to be relevant. I came into the new millennium kicking and screaming. I still love cassettes, compact disks and analog recording devices like my boom box.

However, I want to remain relevant so I have had to embrace technology as never before. We are called to share the gospel by any means necessary. Sure, it's fun to share pictures online of what you cooked for dinner, but you can share what God is doing in your life, just as well. Don't know what to write about? With the click of a button you can share your music, your God-stories, your prayers, encouraging words, take prayer requests, and share your favorite scripture verses.

Pray and ask the Lord to give you ideas on how you can share the gospel online. Partner with other music artists or ministries as well. Use the resources at Babbie Mason Radio (www. babbiemasonradio.com) to promote your music, your books, your radio show or business. Together, if you do what you're called to do and I do what I'm called to do, we can make a world of difference with the love of God.

I have no idea what the future holds. But redefining how we do ministry to remain relevant and keep up with technology is an exciting venture. Maybe you find yourself going through a transition of some kind. Have you lost your job recently and you wonder what your next step might be? Are you nearing retirement age but you don't want to quit working? Do you have a deep desire to do more with your life or make an impact on the global community? Are you recently divorced or widowed?

Reinventing yourself will be necessary. To keep your edge, from time to time you'll have to change the way you do things.

There's an old adage that says, "If you keep on doing what you've always done, you'll keep on getting what you've always gotten." How do you breathe new inspiration into a tired mindset or an old way of doing things? Consider one or more of these ideas.

Change your mind. If the old way of doing things isn't financially rewarding, practically productive or personally gratifying, then find a better way to do it! Get unstuck by changing your mindset. Sometimes our fixed word patterns prohibit open-minded thinking. Instead of instinctively answering a question with, "No..." or "I can't... or "I don't...", consider a more positive, open-ended approach such as, "Let me give this some thought." "What about...." "Where there's a will, there's a way." "I'm open to possibilities. The inspiration I need will come to me." Purposely rid your mind of roadblocks and allow your mind to think freely. This will help ideas to germinate and take off spontaneously.

Remember, you were created by God. He is the author of creativity and He lives in you. He wants to use your creativity and innovation here in the earth. Ask Him to stir up your imaginative abilities enabling you to put your unique stamp on things. Try reading an inspirational book by one of your favorite authors. Watch a good movie. See a live stage play. Take a cooking class or learn to paint.

Collaborate with others. Do something that will stir up your own originality. You'll soon discover new inspirations flooding into your mind. Don't resist. If you don't want to change, you won't. But if you don't, our fast-paced digital world will eventually leave you in the dust. Make the decision that change is inevitable. Then devise a plan to help you adapt. You'll see your creativity abound.

Change your routine. I'll admit, I'm not typically an early riser. But I found if I want to get more done, I need to go to bed earlier and get up before sunrise. Surprisingly, I find I have adjusted well. When I am working on an assignment and I'm in the zone, inspiration will get me out of bed. In the early morning hours my mind is a lot clearer so I'm more creative and a lot less distracted.

That means I'm a lot less stressed and I can get more accomplished before the phone starts ringing with calls and alerts for scheduled appointments. In the early hours I also have more time to invest in myself. My heart and mind are more focused and ready for prayer and time alone with God. I can read my Bible more consistently. I can listen to encouraging messages from my favorite online personalities and even exercise more regularly.

Change your priorities. Dedicate at least an hour a day to doing something to move your ministry or business forward. Make a daily to-do-list and implement a time management system to help you manage your important projects and keep important details from slipping through the cracks. Your to-do list may include returning emails or writing a blog. Make regular social media posts or respond to those who have connected with you. Record an arrangement of a new song demo. Do you need to write thank-you notes? Today could be the day to create a business strategy or pray with friends about an upcoming project. A website is your online headquarters. Do you need to find a designer to help you create that website? Run errands to the post office or print shop. Once or twice a year I find the need to re-write my biography. Maybe it's time you wrote yours. You could make a phone call or two to speak with someone about the possibility of bringing some music to their church or facility. There is always something you can do to move ministry forward.

Change the way you learn. Find a teacher, a mentor or a coach. Want to know more about a particular subject? Take a class.

A coach should be able to help you identify your personal strengths and weaknesses, bringing out your best qualities in order to advance you to the next step in your career.

Great leaders are great learners. Expand your knowledge. Broaden your mind. A teacher, a mentor or a coach can help you do that. The instructor says, "Listen to me. I will teach you the fundamentals of the game."

A mentor could be someone who impacts you indirectly, such as an author whose books you read or a pastor whose sermons you listen to online. A mentor says, "Observe me. You can learn something while you watch me play the game." Or you could be directly impacted by a career or life coach. This could be someone you see by appointment, whether online, over the phone or in person. A coach says, "Let me show you. I'll help you master your game." A coach should be able to help you identify your personal strengths and weaknesses, bringing out your best qualities in order to advance you to the next step in your career. A coach is not a buddy or a therapist, but someone who is interested in facilitating new goals, getting you past small-minded thinking, improving your skills, perfecting your performance and stretching you beyond your boundaries.

A personal coach will assist you in finding your sweet-spot, maximizing your potential. When desiring to advance your career, a personal coach can prove to be more valuable than class instruction.

Change your approach. Try something new. Along the way, I've explored different kinds of occupations. I was a travel guide for a tour bus company. I wrote and delivered the daily news for a local radio station. I was a grocery store bagger and clerk. I worked in a dry-cleaning store. I've sung in a Jewish synagogue during the observance of the Shabbat.

Although these jobs didn't end up being permanent jobs for me, each term of employment contributed something valuable to my life. Some jobs taught me how to interact with the public or how to run an office. Other employment opportunities taught me to improvise on the spur of the moment, sing in another language and appreciate another culture. Some jobs you've had will help to advance your career goals. Others will help pay the rent. But each experience can contribute something to your life story and you can always learn from that.

There's no doubt, God will help you find the right path to success. When you get stuck or find yourself procrastinating, speak to God. Ask Him, "Lord, what is your plan for me." Then speak to the successful self that lies within you. Ask yourself, "How can I implement the plan God has for me?

Change your scenery. To help the creative process flow more easily, make the most of the mundane. Creativity seems to rush in when the mind is at rest. Try a leisurely drive down a country road, taking in the sights. Take a walk and do some bird-watching. Try fishing or gardening. Even performing such mundane tasks as washing the dishes or folding laundry can help your mind to relax. I really

Creativity seems to rush in when the mind is at rest. Try a leisurely drive down a country road, taking in the sights. Take a walk and do some bird-watching. Try fishing or gardening.

enjoy the exercise of browsing through antique stores hunting for old books or hymnals. Any activity where your mind can push out anxious thoughts will set you up to think more clearly and creatively.

I often wonder what kind of things young David thought about when he was away from home for days on end. At night, while he literally counted sheep and gazed up into the night sky to count stars, did he dream of slaying giants or of becoming a king someday?

One thing is for certain, he had a dream hidden away deep in his heart. God knew that dream and He knows the dream that burns in your heart, too. Motivational speaker, Les Brown once said, "Shoot for the moon. Even if you miss, you'll land among the stars." You must believe that! You are enabled, empowered and anointed. Believe this powerful word." I can do all things through Christ Who strengthens me". Philippians 4:13. With the help of God, hard work, a good plan, some creativity and innovation, your dream is one step closer to the launching pad.

CALL TO ACTION

Your assignment today is to dream big in spite of the difficulty you may face. What would happen if you dreamed big like Walt Disney? He filed for bankruptcy seven times, you know. Today, Disneyland is the most visited vacation destination in the world. Would you start a business like Thomas Edison? Some of his inventions were complete failures. But thanks to his persistence, you can flip a switch in a darkened room and stand in a space flooded with light. Would you be an inventor like George Washington Carver? He was born a slave and was denied college entrance because of his race, but later became the first principal and president of Tuskegee Institute. Against all odds, all of these remarkable people made an indelible mark on the world. Now it's your turn. You can't even begin to imagine how big God's plan is for you. God wants to partner with you!

The world is awaiting your contribution. The only thing stopping you is you.

The world is awaiting your contribution. The only thing stopping you is you. Let me pray for you now, that you will find new and creative ways to exercise your gifts.

Dear Father,

I pray for the one that is reading right now, for he or she may sometimes take the easy way out or too often, settle for less. Forgive us for not believing in ourselves. Sometimes we may think we are unqualified for success or that believing in ourselves is wrong. But You have already told us that we can accomplish exceedingly, abundantly, above all that we could ask or think because Your power is at work with in us. That same great power and loving favor that is in Christ Jesus is also in us. With Your ability within us, we can do amazing things. Thank You, Lord!

In Jesus' name,

Amen

Be Creative

CHAPTER 8

BE ABOUT FAMILY

Jesse took a donkey loaded with bread and a jug of wine and a young goat, and sent them to Saul by David his son. Then David came to Saul and attended him; and Saul loved him greatly, and he became his armor bearer. Saul sent to Jesse, saying, "Let David now stand before me, for he has found favor in my sight." l Samuel 16:22-23

A little boy was abruptly awakened during a thunderstorm in the middle of the night. Afraid, he left his bed, ran and jumped into bed with his parents. Interrupted from a deep sleep, his mother assured the little boy that he was not alone. She reminded her son of Jesus' presence and insisted that he go back to bed. Hesitantly, the little boy left his parents' room and returned to his own bed. A few minutes later, streaks of lightning cast dark shadows on the little boy's bedroom walls and thunder rumbled and rolled like an earthquake. The little boy was terrified.

A second time he made a beeline for his parent's bedroom.

Again, his mother assured him that he was not alone. She comforted him, reminding him to pray like he had learned in Sunday school, then insisted he go back to sleep in his own bedroom. Reluctantly, the little boy did as he was told. Before he could crawl into bed the lightning shrieked its bright light and the thunder clapped so loudly the whole house shook. Scared to death, the little fellow ran as fast as he could back to the safety of his parents' bed and nestled in between his mother and father. His mother asked, "Did you remember that Jesus is always with you and He promised He would never leave you - just like you learned in Sunday school?" To that, the little boy replied. "Yes, Mommy. But, right now I need Jesus with skin on!"

While we know God is always with us, we all need the assurance of His presence during challenging times. It's always good to know others are with us, riding out the storms of life, pulling for us to be at our best. At the time I am writing this, Hurricane Harvey is bearing down on the coast of Texas and Louisiana, wreaking havoc with torrential winds and major flooding. While some trees break and splinter easily, the coastal palm tree bends but does not break because it has a deep root system.

> *You can make it through any storm if you have a family that loves and prays for you.*

Like that palm tree, you can make it through any storm if you have a family that loves and prays for you. If you are a believer in Christ Jesus, you are a member of the family of God. We are in this thing together! I believe in you. I'm one of those with skin on. That's why I wrote this book. You have the assurance that you are not alone in this life nor are you alone in ministry. As I write these words I am praying you would always know how vitally important you are to the family of God. The role you play in the body of Christ is important. Stuff and things can be replaced. But you are irreplaceable! Your most important assets are the loving, supportive people around you! To maximize your God-given potential as a family member, cultivate meaningful relationships.

Not only do we represent Jesus 'with skin on', we have skin in the game. I am pulling for you, cheering you on to step into your calling and destiny because what you do really matters. I am praying for your strength as you stand up under the pressure you often experience. Remain strong and immovable in your faith. In difficult times, don't default to your emotions, but trust in God regardless of how you are feeling. I write these words to motivate you to continue to look up in this downcast world.

Stuff and things can be replaced. But you are irreplaceable! Your most important assets are the loving, supportive people around you!

Never forget, you play a major role in furthering God's kingdom. In the spirit, we are running this race together. We have to be determined to do our part and carry our share of the load. And when your brother is hurting, carry his share of the burden as well.

Galatians 6:2 says, "Share each other's burdens, and in this way obey the law of Christ." If we all do what we're called to do, pulling in the same direction, the kingdom of God will be advanced. That's what family does. Do you see how this works?

David's father was slow in recognizing his youngest son's potential. The servant in Saul's palace recognized what David's father had taken for granted. However, this did not stop God's plan from being realized. There was a turnaround in Jesse's attitude the day King Saul sent for David, asking for David's service as his armor bearer. Read 1 Samuel 16:19-22.

So Saul sent messengers to Jesse and said, "Send me your son David who is with the flock." Jesse took a donkey loaded with bread and a jug of wine and a young goat, and sent them to Saul by David his son. Then David came to Saul and attended him; and Saul loved him greatly, and he became his armor bearer. Saul sent to Jesse, saying, "Let David now stand before me, for he has found favor in my sight."

One moment David was tending sheep in a grassy pasture, the next moment he was playing his harp before King Saul in a luxurious palace! One day Jesse's youngest son was a shepherd boy. The next day, Jesse's son was anointed the future king of Israel. Today you may be working a nine to five. Tomorrow may be the day your big dream comes to pass! Don't give up on your dream even if your family members take your dreams lightly. They may write you off, disregarding your dream as a passing fancy. Don't let that deter you from putting everything you have into your work.

Today you may be working a nine to five. Tomorrow may be the day your big dream comes to pass! Don't give up on your dream even if your family members take your dreams lightly.

Your family may be the last ones to get on board. Don't let their discouraging words or lack of support stop you. Put qualified dream-builders around you to help you chart your course. Your family members will come around soon enough. If they don't, they will be the ones who come out on the losing end. Regardless of what it looks like right now, your life-changing moment is just up ahead on the horizon. You may not be able to see it right now, but it is on its way! God's plan for you will come to pass even if others don't recognize your gifts. Proverbs 19:21 says, "Many are the plans in a person's heart, but it is the Lord's purpose that prevails." NIV. You are blessed if you have the support of family to believe in you. Even if you don't, continue to be proactive and find a church, prayer group, or a small group of friends who will provide a place for you to belong. God believes in you and has prepared everything you need for your success.

I know what it is like to have the support of family. Right from the start of this ministry, my entire family has been there to support me. My husband, Charles quit his job after the first year in ministry to help manage the ministry's growth. My children Jerry and Chaz are brilliant. Our oldest son, Jerry is a percussionist and has played on some of my record projects. He also has a degree in audio engineering and has engineered in some of my recording sessions and LIVE concerts, as well as helped to build the infrastructure for our internet radio station. Chaz is a singer-songwriter, producer and session singer. We have written songs and recorded together on numerous occasions and performed on-stage in many LIVE concerts. My mother recorded two songs with me. Stop By The Church, which won a Dove Award in 1997 and God Will Open Up The Windows, was recorded for a video production in 1999. The video of our duet is a YouTube sensation. There are so many highlights along the way. My father passed away in the very early years of ministry when I was just getting started but he and my mother believed in me and paved the way from the very start.

I have other siblings and family members who have supported me through the years as well. Whether through their time, talent, business contacts or physical support, every one of them has contributed something of value to this ministry. Even my grandchildren have been on stage with me! It is the best fun when family is there to enjoy the journey with you. I tell you all of this to celebrate the fact that it is family who made me who I am. They have been there through thick and thin and I owe them a debt of gratitude for their support. The same is true of you.

There are members in your family who have resources your ministry needs. So, involve your family members in your ministry as much and as often as you can. Ask them to help you manage your website or increase your social media presence. Maybe they can accompany you on a trip when you sing, send out a ministry email or critique your stage performance. Other family members can pray for your ministry's success. There is room for everyone in the body of Christ.

While I'm talking about family, let me encourage you to stay connected to your home church. I know it's easy for some people to stay home and not go to church at all. Attending church online is a growing trend. Some people, for one reason or another, are not always able to get to the physical church building. If you are involved in a local church, I commend you! God made us to be people who need other people. To grow and thrive we need to come together, engaging one another. It can be tempting to be a lone ranger, staying to yourself. But there is danger in isolation. Let me share something I saw once on a program called, Wild Kingdom.

To grow and thrive we need to come together, engaging one another. It can be tempting to be a lone ranger, staying to yourself. But there is danger in isolation.

On a sunny, African Savannah, a small impala had wandered away from the herd and far from its mother. Unaware of his surroundings, the impala drifted from his mother's protective gaze. Then a hungry lion laid eyes on the small, helpless animal and preyed upon him. At just the right moment when the mother impala was feeding other young ones, the lion moved in, caught the isolated impala, overtook him and consumed him.

This is a practical picture of a spiritual problem because this is what happens when believers isolate themselves from other believers. They become prey for the adversary.

Listen to what the Bible says in 1 Peter 5:8, "Be sober, be vigilant; because your adversary the devil walks about like a roaring lion, seeking whom he may devour." Then in Hebrews 10:25 it says this. "And let us not neglect our meeting together, as some people do, but encourage one another, especially now that the day of his return is drawing near." It's a fact. You need the local church just as much as the local church needs you.

The internet is a center for connectivity. But in actuality, that connectivity can be a false sense of connection. Although viewing church online is convenient, there is value in being present and accounted for in worship. It is crucial to your spiritual life and the overall vitality of the local church.

Each one of my siblings is unique in their own way. I am in the middle of five and I admire each one of them for their own gifts and talents. Although we are members of the same family, we are all uniquely different. A plethora of gifts and talents are represented in our family. We consist of pastors, teachers, musicians, journalists, community leaders, analytical thinkers, athletes and artists.

While I am aware of my unlimited potential, I also know where my weaknesses lie. Math has never been one of my strengths. Sometimes even simple math problems propose a huge challenge for me. My sister Benita, however, is a math whiz. She worked for IBM for years, building, installing and repairing computers. Benita is now a middle school math coach. She is brilliant and trains teachers to be their best so their students can excel in the area of math.

I figured if anyone could help me with my mathematical ineptitude, she could. So I called her recently and asked her to explain the concept of pi. I've struggled with the concept ever since junior high but I thought maybe this time Benita could help me see the light. From the moment she said, "Pi is a mathematical constant", I got confused and began to zone out. While I heard her explaining what pi is all about, I had visions of pie dancing around in my head and I was counting up all the different kinds of pie I could think of; apple pie, peach pie and sweet potato pie.

While she was talking about irrational numbers, I was thinking how irrational the whole concept of pi seemed to me. All the while, clear visions of a flaky pie crust, filled to the brim with fresh fruits, laced with sugar and spice, began to be a pleasant distraction. I envisioned the steam wafting up between a pretty, latticed crust, baked to golden brown perfection. I drifted in and out of the conversation.

Then she said something about pi being the ratio of a circle's circumference in relationship to its diameter. I said to myself, "Okay, I get that, but much of this pi thing is Greek to me!" As my sister began to explain what a 'ratio' is, I had another vision of perfectly sliced peach pie ala mode on a pretty plate and thought to myself, "I don't care how many times you divide the pie, please save a slice for me. As far as I'm concerned, pie are not squared. Pie are round. Cobbler are squared." Get my drift?

Concerning math, I just don't get some of it. I have actually said concerning my checking account, "I can't be overdrawn. I still have checks left!" But give me a song to sing or an encouraging word to speak to even one person who needs to be uplifted and I come alive! That's what I do. When I sing, I am in my zone! Do you see? Everyone has a part to play in the family.

Television super star, Steve Harvey knows about the power of having a supportive family. When Steve was a student in the sixth grade, his teacher gave the class an assignment: Write down what you want to be when you grow up. Steve, who had a severe stuttering problem, wrote down his dream of being on television.

When the teacher collected the assignment and read Steve's response, she thought his dream was ridiculous, particularly for a boy with a speech impediment. She called Steve to the front of the class and scolded him for not taking the assignment seriously. Then she contacted his parents and reported that Steve had been acting out in class.

Steve knew severe punishment awaited him once he got home from school. His mother was very upset by what Steve had written, but his father was not. "My father said 'What's wrong with that?'" While his parents argued, Steve was sent off to his room. His father came in later and explained to Harvey what to do with his paper. "(He said), 'Take your paper and put it in your drawer. Every morning when you get up, read your paper. And every night before you go to bed, read your paper. That's your paper."

Steve Harvey reveals, "What he told me was a principle of success, that if you write it down and envision it, anything you see in your mind, you can hold in your hand." Through the years Steve Harvey has kept his paper as a reminder that dreams do come true. Steve Harvey reflects. "That little boy with the stuttering problem is on TV seven days a week."

That is the beauty of family that believes in you. We are all different, but all uniquely beautiful and important. You, as a member of your family and as a member of the Body of Christ, must always be supportive of others. There is never room for anger, jealousy, unforgiveness, backbiting, confusion, competition or personal agendas. Family is all we've got. Even when we disagree we can still love each other. I've said for years, "What we are doing here on earth is dress rehearsal for heaven. We must learn to love each other down here so we can live together up there."

My family tree consists of five generations of preachers and pastors that I'm aware of. My great-grandfather, my grandfather, my father, my oldest brother, and his son, were and are preachers and pastors. So I suppose it was easy for me to follow them into ministry.

Family is all we've got. Even when we disagree we can still love each other.

I feel as if I had little or no choice in the matter. Growing up near Detroit, Michigan and being influenced by the music of Motown, there was a time I dreamed of becoming an R&B singer.

I sang in a few bars and clubs around the state of Michigan hoping to jumpstart a career as an R&B singer. But every time I would set foot in a bar or club on a Saturday night, the Holy Spirit would convict me so heavily that I couldn't enjoy myself. Then I'd go to church the next morning and the Holy Spirit would convict me again because of where I had been the night before. I had created a world of compromise. I had too much church in me so I was uncomfortable in the world. And I had too much world in me so I was uncomfortable in the church! What a miserable place to be.

In the fall of 1976 I registered as a student at Spring Arbor College (now Spring Arbor University) in Spring Arbor, Michigan.

I had too much church in me so I was uncomfortable in the world. And I had too much world in me so I was uncomfortable in the church!

My life began to be impacted by other young believers on campus who were living their lives without compromise. One day I sat down at the lunch table, ready to enjoy a cup of piping hot beef vegetable soup. The soup was served in a white Styrofoam cup and a white plastic spoon.

A few minutes into the lunch hour the soup began to grow lukewarm and the oil in the soup began to settle on the surface of the soup, forming oily globules. The orange greasy residue stuck to the sides of the cup and rolled off the plastic spoon. Soon the lukewarm soup was inedible. At that moment, a passage from God's Word came to my mind. My father had used the scripture as a sermon text many times. The passage is found in the book of The Revelation 3:15-16, and written as a letter, to the Church at Laodicea. That day at the lunch table, I knew beyond a shadow of a doubt, God was reading my mail.

"I know your works, that you are neither cold nor hot. I wish you were either one or the other. So, because you are lukewarm - neither hot nor cold, I am about to spit you out of my mouth." NIV

I knew precisely God was speaking to me about my compromising lifestyle. I surrendered my life to Him completely that day. Jesus became my Savior when I was an eight year old girl. But that day as a college junior, Jesus became my Lord.

Here is your take-away.

No compromise. – You've heard the old saying, "If you don't stand up for what is right, you'll fall for anything." That is still true today. I spoke with a lady after one of my concerts lately. She told me she was now in her mid-fifties and she still had not reached any of her ministry and business goals. She confessed, "Starting today, Babbie, it's all or nothing." That's it, my friend. Anything less than your best is compromise. Compromise is like the young man who couldn't decide what side he wanted to fight for during the Civil War. So he wore the trousers of the South and the coat of the North. You know what happened to him? He got shot at from both sides. This is how many people live today. They want to live any old kind of way and still call themselves a Christian. But living a compromising life will short-change you of many blessings. It's not that God is running short on resources. The truth is we don't have the capacity to receive them! God wants to open the windows of heaven on our lives to shower us with blessings, but we are holding up a thimble. Think about your relationship with the Lord. If He seems far away, disconnected and out of touch, guess who moved? Rekindle the flame right now by asking the Holy Spirit to stir up the embers and breathe in your direction. He is ready and waiting to revive your passion when you are ready. Give it all you've got for yourself and for your family.

Think about your relationship with the Lord. If He seems far away, disconnected and out of touch, guess who moved?

No quitting. This is not the time for giving up – this is the time for pressing on. This is not the time to fall under the pressure. Businessman and presidential candidate, Ross Perot said this. "Most people give up just when they're about to achieve success. They quit on the one yard-line. They give up at the last minute of the game, one foot from a winning touchdown." The miracle you've been praying for and working for is not only possible - it's doable. Remember Galatians 6:9 "And let us not get tired of doing what is right, for after a while we will reap a harvest of blessing if we don't get discouraged and give up."

> *"Most people give up just when they're about to achieve success. They quit on the one yard-line. They give up at the last minute of the game, one foot from a winning touchdown."*
> *Ross Perot*

CALL TO ACTION

What does family mean to you? Is there a need for reconciliation in your family today? No matter how difficult, be the first to make the move toward reconciliation and unity. Let love be the motivation. It will make a difference for now and for generations to come. Let's pray together right now for family.

Dear Father,

We praise You for family and for the family of God. Help us to grow strong in You in spite of the storms of life that come against us. Remind us to be there for each other no matter what. We know that nothing works like love. We commit, anew and afresh to be there for family. Thank You for the good things You have in store for us. You are the best Father there is.

With gratitude,

Amen

CHAPTER 9

BE FAITHFUL

"Behold, I have seen a son of Jesse the Bethlehemite who is a skillful musician, a mighty man of valor, a warrior, one prudent in speech, and a handsome man; and the Lord is with him."
1 Samuel 16:18

ℋere's a story I want to share with you.

Day One. I take a walk down Maple Street. There's a big crack in the sidewalk. I trip over the crack in the sidewalk and fall down. I tear a hole in my slacks and scrape my knee. It's difficult to get up. A nice gentleman approaches me, offers me a hand and pulls me up. It costs me 40 dollars to replace my slacks and a trip to the pharmacy to buy bandages for my scraped knee. But it's not my fault.

Day Two. I take a walk down Maple Street. There's a big crack in the sidewalk. It looks familiar but I keep walking. I trip over the crack in the sidewalk and fall down. I tear a hole in my slacks and scrape my knee. It's difficult to get up. A nice gentleman approaches me, offers me a hand and pulls me up. He says to me, "Have we met?" It costs me 40 dollars to replace my slacks and my knee is taking a beating. Still, it's not my fault.

Day Three. I take a walk down Maple Street. There's a big crack in the sidewalk. It looks familiar so I stop to inspect the crack in the sidewalk. While inspecting the crack in the sidewalk I trip over the crack and fall down. I tear a hole in my slacks and scrape my knee. This is painful and it's putting a big dent in my bank account. It's difficult to get up. A nice gentleman approaches me, offers me a hand and pulls me up. He says, "Hey lady, we gotta stop meeting like this." I'm so embarrassed I could kick myself. It costs me 40 dollars to replace my slacks, I am walking with a limp. And it is my fault.

Day Four. I take a walk down Maple Street. There's a big crack in the sidewalk. I know it's there and I see it coming. Although I have to exercise great caution, I walk around the crack in the sidewalk.

Day Five. I walk down another street.

There's a powerful lesson in that story. Someone said that insanity is doing the same thing over and over expecting different results. Old habits are hard to break. They cause us to get stuck. We lose precious time and energy. We may lose hard-earned money and the possibility is great, before it's over, we'll be tremendously frustrated. But, with the right presence of mind, a little determination and when you need it, some help from a friend, we can get unstuck, learn from our mistakes and keep moving ahead toward the goal.

While David made many mistakes, he quickly acknowledged

his sins and made every effort not to repeat them. Saul on the other hand had to learn this lesson the hard way. King Saul had disobeyed the instruction of the Lord on numerous occasions. Saul's lifestyle of disobedience was at the root of his cyclical behavior and eventually led to his death. In a heated battle against the Philistines, Saul was shot by an archer's arrows. Saul took his life by falling on his own sword. Saul's reputation of being unfaithful to God has tainted his legacy to this day. Even after Saul made numerous attempts on David's life, David still highly respected King Saul. After the king was killed in battle, David took Saul's bones and gave them a proper burial.

David endured many seasons in his life. Changes came and changes went but David endured them all. From the day David left home to begin serving King Saul in his palace as personal armor-bearer, to his final days as an old man on his deathbed, David embraced the years with faith and fortitude. He was not perfect by any means, yet he was faithful.

Remember the glowing commendation Saul's servant gave David in 1 Samuel 16:18. "Behold, I have seen a son of Jesse the Bethlehemite who is a skillful musician, a mighty man of valor, a warrior, one prudent in speech, and a handsome man; and the LORD is with him."

Obviously, David could be faithful to God because God was faithful to him. The words King Saul's servant spoke of David, followed him from his youth all the way to his death bed. Read the words again at the end of verse 16. "... and the Lord is with Him."

It was obvious there was something special about David. He could have been an arrogant showman, strutting his stuff around Israel, boasting of slaying Goliath, bragging about his position of royal armor-bearer and personal musician in the king's court. That is a pretty impressive resume.

After all, a lot of people like to mention that kind of stuff in the presence of their counterparts. Ever been in the company of people who like to drop names and talk about where they have been and who they have been with?

David had every reason to boast, yet he executed his assignments with humility, excellence and precision. This ability to deliver wasn't just because David was gifted, youthful or strong. All of that is important. But don't forget that David did what Saul would not. He was obedient to the voice of God. He was faithful to the call of God from his youth to his old age. Even in light of David's obvious indiscretions, he earnestly desired to please God with his life. This keen awareness of the presence of God compelled David to keep short accounts with the Lord. In return, the Lord blessed David with His presence, giving him great favor in times of service, victory over his enemies in times of war, and tremendous approval from the people of Israel.

Even in light of David's obvious indiscretions, he earnestly desired to please God with his life. This keen awareness of the presence of God compelled David to keep short accounts with the Lord.

If you trace David's family tree, you will even find him in the direct lineage of our Savior, Jesus Christ. David's faithfulness and God's favor are a mighty combination. Do you see how the two go hand in hand? This is revelatory. If you want favor from God, remain faithful to God. **To maximize your God-given potential, enduring the tests of time, remain faithful and obedient to God.**

There's a great deal of talk about favor these days. What is favor and how do you obtain it? Favor is the demonstration of God's delight toward a person. Favor is real and tangible evidence that someone has God's approval. When you favor someone, there is a special bond or connection that is established. You want to do good things for that person – you desire to bless them because you love them. You just enjoy being with them. The relationship is not a one-way relationship, but it is reciprocated. God delights in those who take delight in Him. Read what Isaiah 66:1-2 has to say of the Lord.

> *If you want favor from God, remain faithful to God.*

"Heaven is my throne, and the earth is my footstool. Where is the house you will build for me? Where will my resting place be? Has not my hand made all these things, and so they came into being?" declares the LORD. "These are the ones I look on with favor: those who are humble and contrite in spirit, and who tremble at my word." (NIV)

> *Favor is the demonstration of God's delight toward a person. Favor is real and tangible evidence that someone has God's approval.*

God made everything and He needs nothing and no one. Yet, He desires to bless those who are humble and obedient. Understand this, dear friend. God favors those who favor Him with a humble heart and a life of obedience.

Faithfulness is not just an Old Testament directive. The

Apostle Paul inspires us to be loyal, trustworthy and devoted to God in everything. When you were out there in the world, most likely you were sold out to your old ways. You hung out with people who were in the world and you spent your time doing worldly things. Now with that same vigor, you must put all you are into your God-life. Colossians 3:17 says, "Whatsoever ye do in word or deed, do all in the name of the Lord." KJV

It's as if King David and the Apostle Paul are biblical bookends spurring us on to live every day of our lives to the honor and glory of the Lord because every day matters. With that in mind, let me encourage you to remain faithful in the days ahead. As you read these closing stories, think about the importance of remaining faithful.

Remain prayerful. Through the years it has been a privilege of mine to sing at the Brooklyn Tabernacle Church in Brooklyn, New York, and record with their dynamic choir of over 300 voices strong. Pastor Jim Cymbala and his wife, Carol never trained for ministry, but with passion and a calling on their lives, they ventured out in faith to lead a congregation that is a beautiful melting pot of races and cultures. Literally, the congregation is a reflection of the modern day church. In his book, Fresh Wind, Fresh Fire, Pastor Cymbala talks about the power of prayer and how it impacts every part of the church's life. He admits that without prayer, it would be impossible to meet the challenging needs of the urban church's diverse congregation. He says the American church places the emphasis on the sermon, rather than on prayer.

"The sad truth is, in the city where I live – as in Chicago and Philadelphia and Houston, and right across to L.A – more people are turning to crack than to Christ. More people are dipping into drugs than are getting baptized in water. What is going to reverse this tide? Preaching alone will not do it; classes aren't going to do it; more money for more programs won't do it. Only turning God's house into a house of fervent prayer will reverse the power of evil so evident in the world today."

Pastor Cymbala's words continue to remind me that prayer is never a last resort but a first choice. Prayer is our lifeline. It's like the air in our lungs. To remain steadfast in this unstable culture, realize that everything comes as a result of your prayer life; a thriving faith walk, a healthy marriage, a vibrant ministry and anything else that flows out of and into your life.

Remain stable. My dear mother, Georgia Wade lived to be almost 92 years old. She was a very wise woman. My mother's singing voice was my favorite. When I was a child, I remember my mother's clear, pitch-perfect tones lilting through our home like a butterfly in flight. As she was cooking, cleaning or getting ready for church, she was always singing the praises of God. A wife, mother, our church's first lady, choir director and community leader in her own right, she was like E. F. Hutton; when she spoke, everyone listened.

One day in a radio interview I shared with her, she was asked to close the program with some encouraging words. I'll never forget what she said. "When many people are asked how they are doing they will often reply, 'I'm hanging in there.' My mother totally disagreed with that approach to life. She said, "When you're 'hanging in there', you're vulnerable and out of control.

You're at risk to danger and exposed to the elements like a sheet on your grandmother's clothesline. The Bible doesn't say anything about 'hanging in there.' But Ephesians 6:13 says, "Wherefore take unto you the whole armour of God, that ye may be able to withstand in the evil day, and having done all, to stand." My mother continued. "Jesus already 'hung in there' for our hang-ups so we could stand in there, remaining victorious over our circumstances." My mother was so right. Unless I am using this illustration to teach or writing the words to tell a story as lyrics in a song, I've never used the phrase, 'hang in there' again. Just as my mother lovingly admonished me, I recommend that you take the phrase completely out of your vocabulary. You can always find a firm place to stand when you plant your feet on God and His Word.

Remain faithful. Have you noticed when you first start a project everybody is with you, cheering you on? The beginning of a project is exciting and filled with anticipation. But once the project is off the ground and you settle into the daily grind of the routine, those who were with you at the beginning will often fade into the background. Being in the middle of things can be difficult. It's in the middle where you seem to have more month than money. It's in the middle when the car needs repairing and the baby needs a new pair of shoes.

It's in the middle when the phone isn't ringing with new clients. Maybe you know what I'm talking about. Are you in the middle of a difficult marriage and you wonder if your marriage will survive? Are you in the middle of a difficult work assignment and you're not even sure it's worth all the effort? It's possible you are in the middle of a lengthy illness and you wonder if healing will ever come. The only way to make it to the other side is to keep moving forward. Everything you do in the middle makes a difference in the end. You cannot quit. If you quit now, just like

"Jesus already 'hung in there' for our hang-ups so we could stand in there, remaining victorious over our circumstances."
Georgia Wade

a stalled car in the middle of the road, you'll have to be rescued and you'll block others from reaching their destination. James 1:12 says this.

"Blessed is the one who perseveres under trial because, having stood the test, that person will receive the crown of life that the Lord has promised to those who love him." NIV

Those stories I just shared are a real blessing and remind me to just keep moving toward the goal. Even when I wonder if what I'm doing makes any difference, I must believe in my heart that it does.

The only way to make it to the other side is to keep moving forward. Everything you do in the middle makes a difference in the end.

It make a difference for me and for those who depend on me. My good friend and coaching mentor, Dr. Fred Jones said, "Every time you invest in yourself, you are investing in those people who are connected to you." That is powerful! That means when I succeed you succeed. When I grow, you grow. When I make good decisions, you will benefit from those decisions. So, run with people who raise you up, not tear you down. Surround yourself with people who inspire you to aim higher. Don't connect with people just because you like them. Connect with people because they make you better! Your real wealth is not in a program you find online, a paycheck at the end of the month or a product you'll sell at LIVE events. Your real wealth is found in those quality people in your life.

The account of this story is from Bob Reccord's book, Made to Count. He is deeply passionate about impacting lives for Christ.

This really drives home what it means to be faithful in giving God your absolute best, even when it's difficult and inconvenient.

Andy was building a new home. As it often happens, he was having a rather difficult time with the construction crew, subcontractors, installers and suppliers. It was a growing challenge just keeping everyone on schedule. The weather was hot and humid, the project was moving slowly, the boss was frustrated and the men were

"Every time you invest in yourself, you are investing in those people who are connected to you."
Dr. Fred Jones

grouchy. To add to the misery, the port-a-john at the building site reeked with awful odors that caused the crew to gag. The company that serviced it hadn't appeared for days.

Suddenly, blaring music pounded the air as a truck rolled down the street toward the site, filling the block with its rock beat. Everyone's attention shifted as the vehicle slid to a stop in front of the partially completed house. They noticed that it wasn't the regular maintenance man who got out of the truck. Instead, it was a big, burly guy, covered with tattoos, flashing a big smile and singing at the top of his lungs. He greeted the crew, grabbed his equipment and enthusiastically headed for the odoriferous disaster. Before going inside, he yelled across the yard that the former guy had quit and that he would be servicing the unit. He disappeared inside the four-by-six foot cubicle. The rumblings inside the port-a-john grew louder and louder. It almost sounded like he was wrestling a tiger in there.

The construction crew suspended their work temporarily,

their gazes drawn to the spectacle of the port-a-john. A few snickered. They knew the only thing worse than the smell of a port-a-john that hadn't been maintained well was the smell of cleaning that same port-a-john on a hot and humid day. But this guy seemed to stay inside forever. Every man on the site wondered how he could stand it and thought of how quickly they would have raced in and out just to escape the stink.

After a while, the crew noticed something radically different. Mr. Good-natured finally emerged with his smile still intact. "Hey", he said, 'the guy taking care of this for you wasn't doing a very good job. From here on out, I guarantee this will be the best it can possibly be, because I'm here to serve you." With that, he hopped in his truck, grinned, waved, turned on the blaring music once again and began to back out of the driveway. Dumbfounded, one man yelled to the driver, "How can you do that? More important, why do you do that? "Oh, it's simple," replied Mr. Good-natured. "You see, I work for the Lord. And I do every task as though I were doing it for Him. See you next week!" And with that, he drove away, music blaring, singing at the top of his voice, leaving the crew awestruck with their mouths on the ground.

Bob Reccord concluded the story. "Making life count is not so much about what you do as how you do it. And why. And most important, for whom you do it." Do you see how important it is to remain faithful? Even when it's difficult, inconvenient, lonesome and thankless, don't let up. You may think no one notices. Remember people are taking notes on you. Often times they are watching to see if you'll quit. But God is watching to see if you will remain faithful. Ninety-nine percent of your success will be in just showing up. If you continue to make your presence known, not tooting your own horn, but glorifying Jesus with your life, you'll see eternal fruit for your labor. You may not see it all right now, because fruit comes in its season.

Good things come to those who wait. It's possible that much of the fruit that will be produced from your life will remain long after you are gone. While we can count the seeds in an apple, God counts the apples in a seed. We believe in adding and multiplying. God *God is watching to see if you will remain faithful. Ninety-nine percent of your success will be in just showing up.* does exponentially more than we could ask or think. He works in His own way and in His own time. Don't try to figure things out when it comes to watching God work. His ways rarely make sense to our natural minds. You are to be faithful to do what God has called you to do and leave the rest to Him.

Being married to Charles means I watch plenty of football games and football related programs featuring the stories of some of the game's greatest players. One evening we caught an episode of A Football Life: Emmitt Smith. Smith's story is a stellar one. As a child, he grew up in a family that faced financial challenges. As a student at Escambia High School in Pensacola, Florida, he showed tremendous promise.

During his college career at the University of Florida, he set numerous rushing records. He decided to forgo his senior year in college and was drafted into the NFL as a premiere running back for the Dallas Cowboys. He led the Cowboys to back-to-back Super Bowl championships in 1993-94. Along with that, his performance in 1993 earned him the NFL MVP and the Super Bowl MVP that year.

A man of great will, Emmitt Smith exemplifies a tremendous

work ethic that is reflected in his life on and off the field. He said this about life after football. "In this next phase of my life, it's about family. It's business and it's community. I want to maximize my potential and transform the communities that we serve." He went on to say, "Everywhere I've gone, I've left some imprints. And I left that position better than it was before I got there."

While we all can't be Super Bowl MVPs and Hall of Fame champions like Emmitt Smith, we can, like him, be a most valuable asset to those around us, defying the odds that are often stacked against us. Emmitt grew up in a family that struggled financially, but that didn't stop him from working hard and doing his absolute best. He was told he was too small to play in the NFL but that didn't stop him from setting numerous records in his football career and exceeding the expectations of others. He even went on to win Dancing With The Stars! Emmitt is an inspiration to us all, reminding us that we can all be most valuable players to those who depend on us.

Always remember what you do makes a difference. Your family, your children, your co-workers and your church all depend on you for support. Think of yourself like a great tree to those who lean on you. The Bible refers to a great tree in Isaiah 61. Think of what trees do.

Trees provide shade for those who are overheated from the back-breaking toil of life, wearied from the journey. Trees are landmarks, a gathering place for long, engaging conversations where family can tell stories of the past and provide direction for those of the next generation. Trees provide a place to rest for those who still have a long way to go. Trees provide a place for young ones to climb. The higher you help them to ascend, the farther they will see down the road. Trees provide fuel to warm hearts that have become cold and indifferent, hardened because they've been hurt by others. Trees provide shelter for those who have been through a stormy season. Trees provide fruit for those who are hungry and thirsty, needing to be refreshed. And trees provide seeds. Where there are seeds there is hope for a brand new season. People may be impressed by the leaves on your tree, but as they get close enough to inspect your fruit, they will find an abundance of it – fruit in its due season and fruit that will remain to the glory and the honor of God.

They will lean on you and learn from you. They will thank God you are qualified, earning their trust, passing on your faith. Remember Colossians 1:12, "giving thanks to the Father who has qualified us to be partakers of the inheritance of the saints in the light." Remember, Jesus doesn't call the qualified. He qualifies the called. You are qualified because Jesus qualified you. You are validated because He approves of you. You are prepared because He equipped you for the work you must do. I'm cheering you on. Now go and make Jesus look good.

> *You are qualified because Jesus qualified you. You are validated because He approves of you. You are prepared because He equipped you for the work you must do.*

CALL TO ACTION

Do an apple inspection today.
Cut an apple in half and find the seeds. Realize that every living thing comes from a seed – including you. As you hold the seeds in your hand, think of the hope and the future you have all because

of Jesus. Remember James 3:18. "Peacemakers who sow in peace reap a harvest of righteousness."

Let me pray for you now that you will remain faithful to the cause of Christ in the days ahead.

Sweet Father,

Thank You for the privilege of being able to share my heart with this dear friend who has been faithful on the journey. Please take this feeble attempt to speak to the needs of this one who reads these words. You are the ultimate Teacher. Pardon my ignorance, oversights and omissions. Speak to this one in a voice You know they understand. Interpret what I did say and reveal to them what I didn't. Bless the fruit of their hands and their hearts. May everything we do be fueled by a passionate soul, a sound mind and enduring strength. Let me sum this up with some words I wrote years ago in the chorus of a song called, For The Cause of Christ.

For the cause of Christ

I will live my life

I will count my gains as losses

That I might know Him

I find no greater prize

Than my faith in Christ

Treasures and trophies quickly pass

But only what's done for Christ will last

So I will be living my life

Only for the cause of Christ

In Jesus' name,

Amen

NOTES

Introduction

1. *Dr. Myles Munroe, Living With Purpose: The Legacy and Wisdom of Dr. Myles Munroe. Destiny Image Books. 2016. Page 167.*

Chapter One: Be Authentic

1. *Zig Ziglar and Julie Ziglar Norman, Embrace The Struggle, Howard Books. 2009. Page 42*

2. *Charles Swindoll quote - https://www.brainyquote.com/quotes/quotes/c/charlesrs578719.html*

3. *D.L. Moody quote - https://www.brainyquote.com/quotes/keywords/reputation.html*

4. *John Luther quote - www.values.com/inspirations-quotes/7364-good-character-is-more-to-be-praised-than*

Chapter Two: Be Your Best

1. *The definition of the word skill - http://www.businessdictionary.com/definition/skill.html*

Chapter Three – Be Brave

1. *Max Lucado quote - https://www.christianquotes.info/quotes-by-topic/quotes-about-fear*

2. *Jon Acuff quote - https://www.forbes.com/sites/danschawbel/2013/05/09/jon-acuff-why-most-people-dont-reach-their-full-potential-and-how-you-can/#549c9fb67f83*

3. *Dale Carnegie quote - www.brainyquote.com/quotes/dale_carnegie*

Chapter 4 – Be An Encourager

1. *All Rise. Words and Music by Babbie Mason. Copyright 1984. C.A. Music. Admin. by Music Services, Nashville, TN.*

2. *Erma Bombeck quote: https://www.brainyquote.com/quotes/quotes/e/ermabombec106409.html*

Chapter 5 – Be A Leader

1. Bishop Jim Lowe, *Achieving Your Divine Potential*, Bridge Logos. Page 31.

2. Dr. Steve Greene, *Author of Love Leads*. Find the quote from his *Official Book trailer* - https://www.youtube.com/watch?v=EDCLXUmj4vY

Chapter 6 – Be A Servant

1. 1. *He'll Find A Way*. Words and Music by Donna I Douglas. Copyright 1984. Did My Music/ASCAP. Admin. by Clearbox Rights.

2. Marilyn Monroe quote - https://www.brainyquote.com/quotes/marilyn_monroe_498567

3. *Show Me How To Love* – Words and Music by Babbie Mason. Copyright 1988. WORD Music/ASCAP.

Chapter 7 – Be Creative

1. John Maxwell, *How Successful People Think*. Copyright 2000. Center Street Books. Page 25.

2. https://www.brainyquote.com/quotes/quotes/l/lesbrown383867.htm

Chapter 8 - Be About Family

1. *God Will Open Up The Windows of Heaven*, duet with Babbie Mason and her mother, Georgia Wade. You Tube: https://www.youtube.com/watch?v=BaitqrqaXzI

2. Steve Harvey story: http://www.huffingtonpost.com/entry/steve-harvey-gifted-a-tv-every-year-to-the-teacher-who-said-hed-never-be-on-television_us_59b1deaae4b0354e4410c1f9

3 Ross Perot quote - https://www.brainyquote.com/authors/ross_perot

Chapter 9 - Be Faithful

1. Jim Cymbala, *Fresh Wind, Fresh Fire*. Copyright 1997. Zondervan Publishing. Page 83.

2. Bob Reccord, *Made To Count by Bob Reccord and Randy Singer*. W

Fully Qualified

Publishing Group. Copyright 2004. Page 2-3.

3. *A Football Life: Emmitt Smith. https://www.youtube.com/watch?v=OtF47u135eI*

4. *For The Cause of Christ – Copyright 1993. Words and Music by Babbie Mason. Praise And Worship Works/ASCAP. Admin by Word Music, Nashville, TN.*

Fully Qualified

Fully Qualified

DISCOVER WHO YOU ARE AND WHOSE YOU ARE

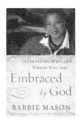

EMBRACED BY GOD – The Book

Embark upon a life-changing journey in Babbie's twenty-one day women's devotional called *Embraced by God*. As Babbie Mason shares her personal story of how she came to understand how very much God loves her, not as a singer or teacher but as His child, she will help you accept that same love and grow in confidence in your faith.

EMBRACED BY GOD: Seven Promises for Every Woman – The Bible Study

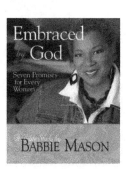

This 8-week study from Babbie Mason will help each woman in your small group know she is loved, accepted, and valued by God. Drawing on her own personal faith journey, Babbie equips women to accept God's unfailing love and claim seven biblical promises that will deepen every woman's relationship with Jesus.

EMBRACE – The Music CD

Inspired by her uplifting book and Bible Study, *Embraced by God*, Babbie Mason presents the companion CD, *Embrace*. Encouraging and God-honoring, each song resonates with the themes of the book, underscoring the powerful message that God loves us just as much as He loves His Son, Jesus. The songs from this CD, serve as a backdrop for Babbie's worship celebration for women, a concert with a distinct message and purpose, called *Embrace: A Worship Celebration For Women.*

Embrace Note Cards

Send some love to a special someone with Babbie Mason's Embrace note cards. Each blank card allows you to write your own sentiments of hope and encouragement. Each box contains twelve cards and envelopes.

Available at: www.babbie.com

EMBRACE: A WORSHIP CELEBRATION FOR WOMEN

EMBRACE: A WORSHIP CELEBRATION FOR WOMEN is a ninety-minute, concert with a specific theme and a distinct purpose. Using her gift for leading women into worship, Babbie Mason invites women to step away from their responsibilities, breathe out, let go of the challenges they face and receive the love, acceptance and affirmation every woman needs. At every Embrace Concert, women experience uplifting worship through music, God-honoring testimonies, the fellowship of Christian sisterhood and a huge dose of encouragement, all in an atmosphere where women can encounter the unconditional love of God.

For more information visit www.babbie.com

LEARN TO LIVE A LIFE OF UNSHAKABLE FAITH

THIS I KNOW FOR SURE-Bible Study

Learn to Live a Life of unshakable faith with the inspiring small group Bible Study, *This I Know for Sure*, by Babbie Mason.

Do you desire a rock-solid faith to believe God for the challenges you are facing, regardless of how you may feel? This 6-week Bible study by award-winning Gospel singer/songwriter and Bible teacher, Babbie Mason challenges you to make up your mind to believe God's Word regardless of your feelings or circumstances.

Whether you are wrestling with questions or fears; struggling in your relationships or facing a health challenge, these principles will enable you to trust God with your doubts, cease your wavering and establish a steadfast faith in the Lord. Each Leader Kit includes: Leader Guide, Participant Book, , DVD, Preview Book, and Music CD.

THIS I KNOW FOR SURE- Book

Be reassured of the promises from God's Word in Babbie Mason's powerful book, *This I Know For Sure*. When life's circumstances attempt to dash your faith, Babbie challenges you to stand on what you know, based on God's Word, not on what you feel. The book is based on the uplifting theme of The Apostle Paul's letter to Timothy in 2 Timothy 1:12, *"I know whom I have believed and am persuaded that He is able to keep that which I've have committed unto Him against that day."*

THIS I KNOW FOR SURE- THE MUSIC CD

Powerful anthems and worship songs will inspire you to press on, as you listen to the music from the companion CD called, *This I Know For Sure*. Enjoy music that lifts your faith and affirms the truths of God's Word. Written around the themes from the book and the Bible study by the same name, the music from this CD will be bolster your faith in these changing times, reminding you that God is trustworthy, He will never forsake you and He has a wonderful plan for your life.

Available at: www.babbie.com

I AM A DAUGHTER OF THE MOST HIGH KING

In Babbie's book, *I Am A Daughter Of The Most High King,* each page delivers a huge portion of fresh insight, heaps of hope, and loads of affirmation, helping women understand more fully, her identity as God's beloved daughter. The book serves as a relevant reminder that as women who are created in the image of God, her identity does not come from her occupation or popular culture. A woman's confidence is not found in her own accomplishments or social status. Every woman, regardless of age or race, in spite of doubts about the future or past mistakes she may have committed, is fully forgiven and totally accepted by God, through His Son, Jesus and has a place in His forever family. All because of Jesus, she is worth it.

Available at: www.babbie.com

THE INNER CIRCLE

THE INNER CIRCLE

Babbie Mason and her husband Charles, host their own exciting music conference called, **The Inner Circle**. Drawing on more than three decades of music ministry and business experience, Babbie and Charles encourage and mentor those desiring to jump-start their own music ministry endeavors. **The Inner Circle** is a power-packed event where attendees learn vitally important spiritual and practical tools, tips and techniques for launching music ministry, songwriting, recording music on a budget, Internet marketing techniques, vocal care, stage presence, radio promotion and networking with peers. Babbie features many of her friends in the music industry who join her for this encouraging weekend conference. Hear from professionals in the industry including producers, songwriters, arrangers, vocal coaches, entertainment attorneys, web masters, and Christian artists. Guests have included award-winning gospel singer, Helen Baylor, Carol Cymbala (director of the Brooklyn Tabernacle Choir), Charles Billingsley, Morris Chapman, Pastor William Murphy, Kenn Mann, Donna Douglas, Eulalia King, Cheryl Rogers and more.

Find out more at www.babbie.com

BABBIE MASON RADIO

Log on to www.babbiemasonradio.com to hear beautiful music and encouraging words 24 hours a day. Access the internet radio station from your desktop, laptop or any mobile device. Hear Babbie's timeless music, the stories behind her original songs, her encouraging messages, and back-stage interviews from the road. The online station features your favorite Christian music genres, including Contemporary Christian, Praise And Worship, Urban Gospel and Gospel Music Classics from back in the day.

You will hear great music on Babbie Mason Radio along with popular Christian programs featuring your favorite radio personalities, exciting interviews as well as upbeat stories and testimonies. As a mentor to Christian music upstarts, Babbie embraces the music and life-stories of independent Christian artists from around the globe – those singers and songwriters who record and promote their music independently of a major record label. Also at Babbie Mason Radio, we endeavor to support the ministries of self-published Christian authors – those Christian authors who write, publish and promote their own books independently of a major book publisher. We consider it a real honor to help Christian music artists and authors get the word out about their music and books, providing an online community where they are validated and celebrated on a global platform.

Whether you are a fan of great Christian music, enjoy relevant interviews, or news and encouraging programs from a Christian perspective, you'll find Babbie Mason Radio exciting, encouraging, informative, family-friendly and God-honoring. Babbie Mason Radio is where you'll find hope in Christ at the click of a button.

www.babbiemasonradio.com

BABBIE'S HOUSE

Babbie Mason takes her timeless music and uplifting message to television on her TV talk-show, **Babbie's House**. On the air for twenty years, Babbie features a variety of guests; singers, songwriters, authors, preachers, community leaders, and everyday people with extraordinary stories. With her own brand of warmth, wit and wisdom, Babbie sings on each show and engages guests in informative and upbeat conversation. Guests have included Mary Mary, Israel Houghton, David and Tamela Mann, Kay Arthur, Liz Curtis Higgs, Candi Staton, Larnelle Harris, Jeanette Marie Hawes of the Emotions, Vernessa Mitchell and many more. Seen all over the continental United States and online. Check local listings.

www.watc.tv
www.babbie.com

Mentoring And Coaching

Babbie Mason is dedicated to teaching, mentoring and coaching those who desire to launch their dream as a singer, songwriter, author or public speaker. Receive personal, industry-level instruction from Babbie Mason, an award-winning singer, songwriter, author and conference speaker. Opportunities for instruction are available in a number of different settings from the exciting weekend music conference for Christian singers and songwriters called, The Inner Circle. Intensive small group sessions are available. For maximum impact, one on one coaching in the areas of songwriting, self-publishing and artist development are also available. Designed for those who want to take their gifts and talents to the next level, Babbie is passionate about pouring into the lives of others to maximize their God-given potential. For more information contact Babbie at babbie@babbie.com

www.babbiemasonradio.com

WHJD

www.WHJD4you.com

WHAT HAS JESUS DONE FOR YOU? WHJD is an exciting evangelism campaign designed to help believers in Jesus Christ make a great commotion of the Great Commission. We invite you to post your God-story on www.WHJD4you.com to help promote the message of the gospel and tell the world about the difference Jesus Christ makes in your life. What Has Jesus Done (WHJD) for you? Given you a brand new start? Breathed new life into a failed marriage? Delivered you from the prison of addiction? Healed you of disease? Reconciled your family? Restored your finances? Whatever the circumstances, every believer in Christ Jesus has a unique God-story to tell and a dynamic faith that deserves to be shared with the world. No story is insignificant or ordinary. If Jesus has changed your life then it's a really big deal! You can begin right where you are by sharing your God-story on our website at www.WHJD4you.com. Celebrate what Jesus has done for you by sharing your God-story today. When you post your story on our website, take time to read the powerful stories of others, too. Then help us spread the word about WHJD by connecting with us on all of our social media platforms!

www.WHJD4you.com

FACEBOOK: WHJD4you

WHJD™

University Advancement

Spring Arbor University is a community of learners distinguished by our lifelong involvement in the study and application of the liberal arts, total commitment to Jesus Christ as the perspective for learning and critical participation in the contemporary world. – The Concept

At Spring Arbor University we are committed to fostering a diverse learning environment that values the dignity of every human being. SAU takes seriously the nurturing of our Christian community so that all students regardless of their background are respected. Our desire is to be a community that reflects the breadth and diversity of God's creation.

Babbie Mason, 1978 graduate of SAU, valued her opportunity to study here. In her concerts, I have heard her share of the multiple ways in which God used her Spring Arbor University experience to continue molding her into the person she knew He wanted her to become. The individual attention she received from professors, the weekly spiritual boost she received from chapel, and the loving care provided from the greater community endeared her heart and life to this place.

As a result, she endowed The Babbie Mason Minority Music Scholarship Fund. It is a fund which annually provides scholarships for minority students majoring or minoring in music. Babbie is passionate about assisting students as they prepare for life in Christ. She biennially presents a concert in Spring Arbor where all proceeds from the concert are added to the scholarship.

If you would like to assist Babbie in growing this endowed fund, you may do so by providing a gift of cash, stock, an insurance policy, a charitable gift from a donor advised fund or from your IRA. Checks should be made payable to: Spring Arbor University. On the memo line, please write "The Babbie Mason Minority Music Scholarship Fund." You may also go online to www.arbor.edu/give and designate your contribution to her scholarship. If you desire to give through an insurance policy, from a stock gift transfer, a donor advised fund, or from your IRA please contact Spring Arbor University at (517)-750-1200 and ask to speak with the Director of Planned Giving. This person will be able to help guide you in completing your gift.

God has blessed and used Babbie. We are proud to claim her as one of our own. Our prayer is that she will continue to minister in Kingdom building. May she always know God's peace, protection, and provision. Thank you, Babbie. We love you.

With a merry heart,

Danny Lacy

Danny Lacy
Director of Planned Giving
Spring Arbor University

About The Author

$\mathcal{T}$he name Babbie Mason is synonymous with creative excellence in the Christian community. She is an American Christian singer-songwriter and the recipient of two Dove Awards for her singing and songwriting abilities. A host of other awards and recognitions line her walls, including eleven Dove Award nominations, nominations for the Grammy, the Stellar and the Emmy. She has also received nominations for Female Vocalist of the Year and Songwriter of the Year. In 2010 Babbie Mason was recognized for her contributions in Gospel music upon her induction into The Christian Music Hall Of Fame.

A native of Jackson, Michigan, Babbie is the daughter of a Baptist pastor. She learned to serve others while developing her musical skills as pianist and choir director at the Lily Missionary Baptist Church, the church her father founded and pastored for 39 years. Demonstrating exceptional musical abilities early in life, she became the church's full-time pianist and choir director by age nine. Those humble beginnings paved the way for a ministry that has taken Babbie Mason across the globe where she has encouraged the hearts of young and old alike in churches, conferences and corporate conventions for over three decades. Babbie has appeared on stage at events such as Billy Graham Crusades world-wide, Bill Gaither Homecoming events, The Grammy Awards and Carnegie Hall. Her gifts and talents have allowed her to share the platform with such notable people as Presidents Carter, Ford and Bush, Former First Lady Barbara Bush, Bishop T.D. Jakes, NBA legend, Michael Jordan and General Colin Powell.

A gifted singer and versatile songwriter, her timeless compositions can be found in multiple genres of Christian music, including Contemporary Gospel, Traditional Gospel, Urban Gospel and Southern Gospel music. Some of the nation's most prominent Christian artists and groups have recorded her compositions, including CeCe Winans, Albertina Walker, Al Green, Larnelle Harris and The Brooklyn Tabernacle Choir. Her compositions have been translated in over twenty languages, and many are considered modern day church classics. She has garnered two ASCAP Awards and composed numerous radio singles such as, All Rise, With All My Heart, Each One, Reach One, Trust His Heart, Standing in the Gap, God Will Open Up The Windows and Love Is The More Excellent Way. You will find her songs among the pages of the world's most famous composers in church hymnals, musicals and octavos. Her songs have been featured on television and in motion pictures, such as Show Time At the Apollo, and Denzel Washington's blockbuster, Déjà vu.

A college professor, TV talk show host of Babbie's House seen on DirecTV, author of six books, and a recording artist with twenty-four recorded music projects to her credit, Babbie Mason shows no signs of stopping. In an effort to promote Christian music, and specifically, the music and life-stories of independent Christian music artists and authors, in 2014 Babbie launched BabbieMasonRadio.com, an online radio platform. She and her husband Charles, make time to mentor up and coming Christian singers, songwriters and authors at The Inner Circle, a weekend music boot camp they host together.

For more than three decades Babbie Mason has been known all over the world for her contributions of encouraging words and beautiful music. However, she remains humble, recognizing that her blessings come from above. It is no wonder Babbie Mason is blessed with a plethora of talents. She does not hesitate to share her gifts with the world. And those gifts are still making room for her. Whether singing, composing music, teaching students, hosting her TV show, running an online radio station, speaking to women or sharing her heart through her books and women's Bible studies, her heart shines through like a bright star. When you meet her, you'll meet a friend with a contagious love for God and people.

The parents of two adult sons and two perfect grandchildren, Babbie and Charles Mason live on a farm in Georgia.

www.babbie.com

www.babbiemasonradio.com

Fully Qualified